Compact Disc
Troubleshooting & Repair

ℋ

HOWARD W. SAMS & COMPANY/HAYDEN BOOKS

Related Titles

John D. Lenk's Troubleshooting & Repair of Audio Equipment
John D. Lenk

Video Cameras: Theory and Servicing
Gerald P. McGinty

VCR Troubleshooting & Repair Guide
Robert C. Brenner

Troubleshooting with the Oscilloscope, Fifth Edition
Robert G. Middleton (revised by Joseph J. Carr)

Electronic Test Instruments: A User's Sourcebook
Robert Witte

How to Read Schematics, Fourth Edition
Donald E. Herrington

How to Read and Interpret Schematic Diagrams
J. Richard Johnson

John D. Lenk's Troubleshooting & Repair of Microprocessor-Based Equipment
John D. Lenk

CD-I and Interactive Videodisc Technology
Steve Lambert & Jane Sallis

For the retailer nearest you, or to order directly from the publisher, call 800-428-SAMS. In Indiana, Alaska, and Hawaii call 317-298-5699.

Compact Disc
Troubleshooting & Repair

Neil Heller
Thomas Bentz

HOWARD W. SAMS & COMPANY
A Division of Macmillan, Inc.
4300 West 62nd Street
Indianapolis, Indiana 46268 USA

FIRST EDITION
SECOND PRINTING—1989

International Standard Book Number: 0-672-22521-2
Library of Congress Catalog Card Number: 87-62221

Acquisitions Editor: *Greg Michael*
Manuscript Editor: *J. L. Davis*
Illustrator: *T. R. Emrick*
Cover Artist: *James R. Starnes*
Compositor: *BMEP, Inc., Zionsville, Ind.*

Printed in the United States of America

Technics is a division of Matsushita Electric Corporation of America (MECA).

Contents

Preface

The technological advancements made in sound recording/ reproduction in the last few years have been remarkable. Today, if you visit a local record store, you will find three dominant formats of prerecorded music: the cassette tape, the conventional LP record, and the compact disc (CD). Repeat visitors will also note how the CD is competing for, and actually achieving, more and more space on the display shelves.

Compact disc players have been available now for about six years, but the excitement has really just begun. The CD format has started to flourish within the last three years. Its rate of growth, at this point, is by all means impressive. The CD represents the first successful influx of digital audio into the consumer market. More and more consumers are realizing that as we move toward the 90s, digital sound is the way to go. The quality of sound reproduction from a CD is far superior to that of the previous consumer-oriented sound-storage mediums.

The CD systems utilize digital recording technology, laser, and laser-optics technology, and sophisticated schemes of compensating for any possible flaws that may be encountered in playback. In all, the CD system is a well designed, well thought out method of sound storage for large-scale mass production.

More and more manufacturers are producing more and more players. The demand is there, and it isn't expected to wane. Perhaps the last new consumer item to make such a splash was that of the home video cassette recorder, in Beta and VHS formats. These units are extremely popular, and have themselves generated new businesses, such as video movie rental stores, and small-scale production companies. Along with this wide acceptance, it was correctly anticipated that the need for service would increase. Consequently, more technicians are being trained on VCR repair in order to keep up with the times. Additionally, more technicians are able to specialize just in VCR repair because of the large number of units that are in the field. The servicing industry has grown and met the needs of the VCR-buying public.

But what about the CD-player-buying public? It's not very unusual for individual consumers to have two (or more) CD players, especially now, since the attractive portables are available. All these players will probably have to be serviced at one time or other, and the consumer expects to have competent service readily available.

The aim of this book is to give the reader, whether he or she is a technician, engineer, hobbyist, audiophile, or simply an interested music lover, some essential background in the science of sound recording/ reproduction, and to develop this background into an understanding of the complete CD system. Also, detailed circuit descriptions, troubleshooting procedures, and alignment procedures are included to serve as specific examples of what to do when you are confronted with a malfunctioning CD player. Stated differently, this book is designed to teach the basics of the CD system, and to help you in your servicing efforts.

The authors believe that this book is both comprehensive and enlightening. They hope you will find that it serves its purpose, and that it becomes a permanent part of your reference library.

NEIL HELLER
THOMAS BENTZ

Acknowledgments

Since the compact disc system is really a new audio reproduction format, a large part of the technical information about the system came directly from various manufacturers. The service and/or training manuals from North American Philips, Sony, Pioneer, and Panasonic/Technics served the authors well in the area of circuit explanations, schematics, alignments, and CD system fundamentals. Various audiophile-oriented magazines, including *Stereo Review, Digital Audio,* and *Audio*, were also very helpful, as were publications from the Audio Engineering Society (AES). The books *Principles of Digital Audio* (Sams), by Ken C. Pohlmann, *Audio Cyclopedia*, second edition (Sams), by Howard Tremaine, and *Handbook for Sound Engineers* (Sams), by Glen Ballou, proved to be very valuable sources. And thanks are in order to Mr. Harry Foulds, National Training Manager for Matsushita Services Company (Panasonic/Technics/Quasar) for access to the training manual for the Technics SL-P2 and the training video tape *The Basics of Compact Discs*.

Without such references, the authors could never have produced any work of this nature.

1

The Audio Signal

The goal of any piece of audio equipment is to reproduce sound with perfect fidelity to the original sound. In concept, this is a good goal to strive for. In reality, any type of electronic equipment has a number of limitations which prevent the reproduced signal from being an exact duplicate of the original.

Since the introduction of the phonograph record, electronics manufacturers have attempted to create more convenient and error-free methods of signal reproduction. This search for the perfect method of audio reproduction has gone from the record to audio recording tape and now to the digital audio disc. Tape was an improvement on records in that it allowed for home recording as well as playback. Its development from large, reel-to-reel machines to cassette form permitted easier recording as well as mobility. While improving handling features, tape offered little in improved quality. As a result, both the audio record and audio tape continued to exist side by side. The introduction of the digital audio represents perfection and the possibility of combining high-quality signal reproduction, mobility, and self-recording.

Even though all three forms of audio reproduction use different methods to reproduce sound, each is an attempt to improve on the previous method by correcting its deficiencies. An understanding of digital audio disc systems begins by understanding the formats that preceded it. All have in common the goal of re-creating sound.

IN THE BEGINNING: SOUND

As previously noted, the goal of any kind of electronic sound equipment is to re-create a quality which closely matches that of the original source. The ability to achieve this is based on a combination of understanding the concept of sound and the limitations of electronic equipment to re-create it.

THE CONCEPT OF SOUND

Sound is the effect produced by a displacement of pressure on the surface of an object. When a sound is produced, say by banging on a drum, the skin of the drum displaces the air around it. First, the action of the impact expands the drumskin,

1

compressing the air on the other side and causing a buildup of air pressure. This area of "high" pressure is then transmitted to the next layer of air. After the drumskin expands, it then starts to retract, causing the area of high pressure in front of the skin to become low. Until the drumskin returns to its resting position, a rhythmic, but decreasing amount of pressure will be created in front of the drum, as shown in Fig. 1-1. In order for these high- and low-pressure changes to be heard, the sound wave must reach the human ear. Here, these changes in pressure will cause the eardrum to vibrate in a manner similar to the drumskin. The human brain will then interpret the vibration of the eardrum and convert it into a recognizable sound.

Constructing Sound: The Sinusoidal Wave

If we were to plot the changes in pressure caused by striking the drum, we would find that each rise in pressure was followed by a corresponding decrease. The cycle is complete when the signal reaches its same strength as its starting point, after going through its positive and negative halves. By returning to the same potential as its starting point, the signal is said to have trans-

gressed through 360° (just as we describe a circle). The result is known as a *sinusoidal wave*, which is shown in Fig. 1-2.

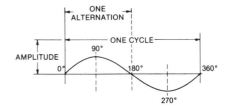

Fig. 1-2. Development of a sinusoidal wave.
(From Howard Tremaine, Audio Cyclopedia, *p. 15)*

Sound has two characteristics, first, amplitude, or signal strength, and second, frequency, or the time it takes the sine wave to complete one full cycle. Frequency indicates the number of times a sine wave occurs during a period of one second. If a sine wave occurs 10 times per second, it has a frequency of 10 cycles per second, which is more commonly referred to as 10 hertz.

Frequency and the Quality of Sound

The frequency of the audio sine wave determines not only what we hear, but also if we hear the sound at all. As frequency increases it changes

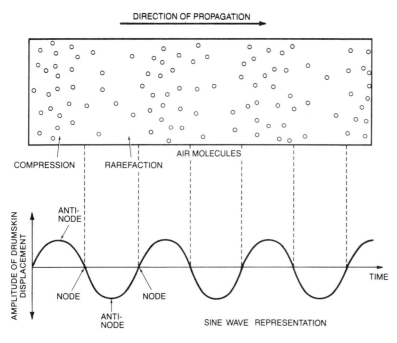

Fig. 1-1. Sound propagation.
(From Ken Pohlmann, Principles of Digital Audio, *p. 18)*

our interpretation of the sound. Low-frequency sounds have a bass quality, while high-frequency sounds have a sound that corresponds to treble. As a result, changing the frequency of a sound changes its pitch. It is generally accepted that the human ear can hear sounds from a range of 20 to approximately 20 000 hertz (this is considered the maximum audio range, so that not all people are able to perceive sound in this wide range).

Because our hearing deteriorates with age to upper levels of 15 000 to 18 000 hertz (or less), the maximum limits of human hearing are actually determined by the hearing range of a young child.

CREATING THE AUDIO SIGNAL: THE RECORD

From a historical prospective, audio signals were first re-created by means of records (discs). Then came magnetic tape and at present we have the laser disc. Each has been an attempt to improve on the signal fidelity as well as resolve the faults of the previous format.

The Audio Record (Disc)

In a record the signal information is contained within the grooves, which are cut into the record's surface. For stereo, right- and left-channel information is contained in the left and right walls of the groove, as shown in Fig. 1-3. The dimensions of the left and right walls determine the angle, or depth, of the groove. To create the master record disc (from which mass-produced copies are made) audio signals are fed into a series of coils, one set for the right channel and one for the left channel. Fig. 1-4 shows these coils, which cause the cutting stylus to move in proportion to the incoming signal. As a result the shape of the groove is a geometric representation of the signal. As with any electromechanical device the cutting stylus may not respond in exact accordance with the audio signal, and could therefore produce frequencies not contained in the original signal. If left uncorrected, the cutting

needle would carve these unwanted frequencies into the disc's surface. To prevent this condition the series of feedback coils is found close to the cutting stylus. The motion of the cutting stylus induces a voltage into these coils which is fed back to the input amplifier 180° out of phase. This voltage tends to correct the stray movements of the cutting stylus.

Fig. 1-3. Stereo grooves on a conventional record. *(Courtesy Stanton Magnetics, Inc. From Glen Ballou,* Handbook for Sound Engineers, *p. 892)*

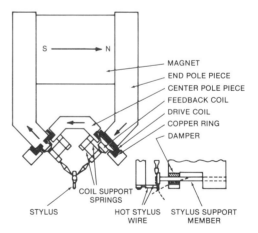

Fig. 1-4. Simplified cross-sectional view of Westrex stereophonic cutting head. *(Courtesy Westrex Corp., Division of Mitsubishi Pro Audio Group. From Glen Ballou,* Handbook for Sound Engineers, *p. 834)*

The physical structure of the cutting stylus also helps to determine the purity of the signal cut into the disc's surface. The geometry of the wall is a physical representation of the input audio signal. The cutting stylus must be able to handle a variety of changing conditions in order to inscribe a range of signals between 20 and 20 000 hertz. Groove geometry is dependent on the amount of physical groove displacement. This, in turn, is determined by the acceleration and velocity of the cutting stylus where it contacts the disc. The cutting stylus and its magnetic drive-coil assembly (known as the cuting head) have a physical characteristic called *constant velocity*. Simply stated, this means that the stylus will travel farther from its resting point when cutting low frequencies than it does when cutting high frequencies (see Fig. 1-5). This can translate to a problem in playback, where higher frequencies would be attenuated. An additional problem exists in the total amount of recording time, because the space between grooves would have to be increased to accommodate the low-frequency excursions. Increased spacing between grooves costs more and reduces recording time. To overcome this, a recording system was adopted to make the cutting stylus behave in a more "constant-amplitude" fashion. Fig. 1-6 shows the stylus displacements obtained. This system preemphasized (or boosted) higher frequencies during the cutting process and deemphasized (or reduced) them during playback. When compared, the preemphasis and deemphasis effects on the signal are inversely proportional to each other. The net effect provided for a reasonably flat amplitude over the audible frequency range. By selecting certain frequencies to check the relationship between constant velocity and constant displacement the record industry was able to develop a standard that ensures that records produced in one country will be compatible on turntables produced in another.

Reproduction of the signal occurs when the record player's stylus rides along each wall of the groove, as shown in Fig. 1-7. As it travels in the groove, the needle vibrates according to the pattern created in the groove. The signal's amplitude variations are determined by the physical structure of the groove. In order to save space on the disc, the grooves are narrower and closer together when the overall signal amplitude

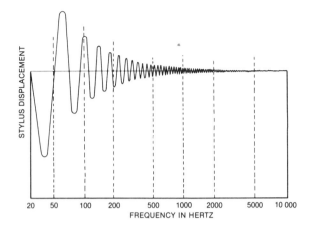

Fig. 1-5. Constant-velocity characteristic of a cutting head. *(From Howard Tremaine,* Audio Cyclopedia, *p. 699)*

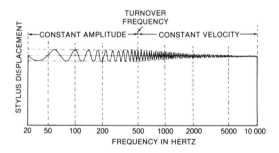

Fig. 1-6. Desirable characteristics of a magnetic cutting head. *(From Howard Tremaine,* Audio Cyclopedia, *p. 700)*

Fig. 1-7. Playback stylus in a stereo groove. *(Courtesy Stanton Magnetics, Inc. From Glen Ballou,* Handbook for Sound Engineers, *p. 887)*

is low, and farther apart when the overall signal level is greater.

Groove widths also differ, depending on the speed of the disc. For long-playing records which rotate at 33$^{1/3}$ revolutions per minute (rpm), the groove width is approximately 2 millimeters. For shorter-duration records, which rotate at 45 revolutions per minute, groove widths between 3 to 3.5 millimeters are common. The geometry of the groove causes the playback stylus to vibrate during the playback process, just as the cutting stylus did during recording. The vibrating playback stylus is a part of the playback cartridge. If the cutting head can be considered to be a motor (and it is), then the playback cartridge is a generator. The vibrating stylus will cause a similar vibration between a magnet and coil assembly inside the cartridge (crystal cartridges are now obsolete). This coil (coils for stereo) will deliver an electrical output signal, that is, a re-creation of the original audio signal used for cutting.

Problems of Conventional Audio Discs

The quality of the audio signal is dependent on the quality of the groove and on the pickup stylus. Any change to the structure of either the groove or the pickup stylus will be amplified and result in distortions. Dirt and damage to the groove can change the characteristics of the groove wells. More commonly, both the stylus and groove exhibit wear with time due to the action of the stylus scraping against the surface of the groove wall. Stylus wear can be corrected by replacement of the stylus. Usually the only way to repair a worn record is to replace it.

Another enemy of audio discs is variation in temperature. The plastic material that makes up the composition of the disc will expand and contract with varying temperature. This changes the geometry of the grooves, distorting the output. The effect is known as *warping*. Uneven travel of the stylus over the record's surface will result in a loss of output signal amplitude or skipping of a complete audio track. The loss of stylus-to-record contact caused by minimal rec-

ord warping can usually be compensated by increasing the pressure of the needle against the record. The trade-off is that the increase in pressure causes more record and stylus wear. If the warping is too great, the only solution is to replace the record.

Although record cutters did exist at the consumer level (but on a very small scale), the need to have a reusable recording medium helped lead to the development of recording and playback audio signals on magnetic tape.

RECORDING AUDIO SIGNALS ON TAPE

Magnetic tape recording works on the principle of retained magnetism. When a magnetic field is applied to a metal object, such as iron and steel, the particles that compose the metal take on the polar properties of the applied magnetic field. As a result, these particles will align themselves with the north and south poles of the field. This alignment is known as *flux density*, and it is a result of the intensity of the applied magnetic field. Given that the metallic properties of an object are constant, increasing the intensity of the applied magnetic field increases the flux density in the object. The ability of an object to accept a magnetic field is known as *permeability*. This acceptance continuously increases until all the metal particles in the object have aligned themselves with the magnetic field. This condition is known as *saturation*.

Applying the signal to tape is only one-half of the process. Fig. 1-8 shows how a varying signal creates a varying magnetization in the tape. The ability to record signals on tape depends on how well the magnetic tape retains the applied signal after the magnetic field is removed. This quality of a metal is known as *retained magnetism*. Many metals, such as aluminum and nickel, require extremely strong magnetic fields to produce even small amounts of retained magnetism.

The differences in audio tape are due to the differences in materials. Each of the types of

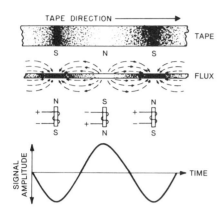

Fig. 1-8. Basic principle of magnetic recording. *(From Howard Tremaine,* Audio Cyclopedia, *p. 757)*

tape–normal, CrO_2, and metal tape–differ in their ability to reproduce signals based accepting and retaining a magnetic field.

Transferring the Signal to Tape

The purpose of any piece of audio reproduction equipment is to reproduce a signal which resembles that of the original input signal. The process of magnetic recording, however, limits the exact reproduction of the incoming audio signal. The degree of signal reproduction accuracy is related to the method used to transfer signals to and from the tape.

The audio information is applied to the tape by means of a small electromagnet, known as the *audio head*. In order to provide the maximum magnetic field intensity at the point where the tape contacts the head, the individual poles of the electromagnet are positioned close together, but at no point do they touch, as shown in Fig. 1-9. This head "gap" area will provide a high reluctance (signal resistance) to the applied signal. As the alternating-current (ac) signal flows through the coils of the audio head it causes a magnetic field to develop between the two poles of the head. During the time the positive part of the cycle is present, the magnetic field builds up. During the negative portion the field collapses and builds in the opposite direction. This changing state of magnetism is responsible for creating the magnetic flux. Where the tape

contacts the head, as in Fig. 1-10, the magnetic path is complete and that section of the tape will exhibit characteristics equal to the direction and intensity of the applied magnetic flux.

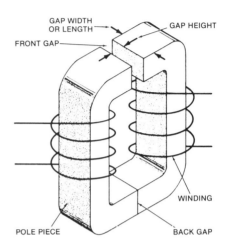

Fig. 1-9. Basic construction of a magnetic recording head. *(From Howard Tremaine,* Audio Cyclopedia, *p. 782)*

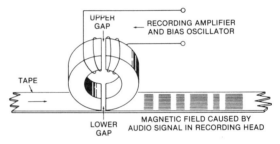

Fig. 1-10. Recording a magnetic pattern on tape. *(From Howard Tremaine,* Audio Cyclopedia, *p. 763)*

The method of using an alternating current to record the audio signal presents our first system limitation. As the audio signal is composed of changing polarity, the tape speed must be fast enough to allow enough space on the tape to record a complete cycle. If the tape speed is too slow, both the positive and negative portions of the audio cycle will be recorded in the same area. The result will be a loss of part of the signal as the negative portion cancels out part of the positive cycle. In a worst case condition, if a complete cycle was recorded in exactly the same tape area the result would be zero. Fig. 1-11 shows the gap effects for relatively low and high frequencies. On the other hand, too high a tape speed would result in high tape consumption, which is particularly important in the construction of smaller tape formats, such as the common Philips audio cassette. So, tape speed is a compromise between moving the tape quickly enough to provide space to record frequencies between 30 and 20 000 hertz and slow enough to provide a reasonable length of recording. For standard audio cassettes the tape speed is $1^7/_8$ inches per second (ips), or 4.76 centimeters per second.

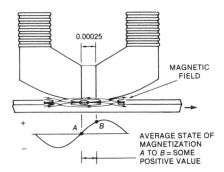

(A) Playing back a relatively low frequency.

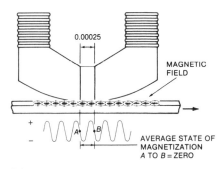

(B) Playing back a frequency that is too high.

Fig. 1-11. Gap effects of a playback head for low and high frequencies. *(From Howard Tremaine, Audio Cyclopedia, p. 758)*

We face similar problems with passing signals through the audio head. Some losses occur in the head itself from internal currents (not a part of the audio signal) within the structure of the audio head. This current increases with frequency and disperses itself in the form of heat. This effect can block the actual transfer of audio signals.

The Head Gap

The audio signal is transferred in the area of the head gap. The size of the head gap also deter-

mines the frequency of the signal that can be applied to the tape. If the physical gap of the head is big enough to allow the complete cycle of the signal to pass, the result would be the same as recording a complete cycle on the same tape area. The result of a complete cycle in the gap area would be zero. As a result the physical gap size of the head can only be a physical size equal to that of the electronic distance of one-half the highest recorded frequency.

The highest energy transfer contained within the gap can therefore be characterized by the following formula:

$$G = \frac{\lambda_h}{2}$$

where

G = size of gap,
λ_h = tape wavelength of highest recording frequency.

The Role of Bias

In order to achieve a proper recording, the complete range of audio frequencies from approximately 20 to 20 000 hertz must be recorded on the tape without distortion. However, the magnetic properties of conventional tape are not linear. That is, as the input signal increases above zero, the magnetization starts to increase at a low rate. As the input signal increases further, the magnetization rate increases, and so on to a point where the tape becomes "saturated" and no magnetization increase will occur despite an increase in the input audio signal. This same characteristic is demonstrated as the input signal drops–the magnetization drop is not linear. This characteristic response can be plotted on a graph and becomes the identifiable *B-H* curve, which is shown in Fig. 1-12. Applied directly to the tape, the audio signal will create a distorted magnetic alignment on the tape, resulting in signal distortion. In order to prevent this, a high-level, high-frequency signal is mixed with the audio prior to being applied to the heads. This bias signal shifts the recording point to a linear portion of the audio head and tape magnetization curve. As a result the magnetic particles on the tape are aligned (or realigned if a previous signal was present on tape) to a state that allows maximum acceptance of a new signal with minimum distortion and noise. Fig. 1-13 shows how this is done. As each different type of tape, normal, CrO_2, and metal, has different linear signal transfer points, the bias for each of these types of tape differs.

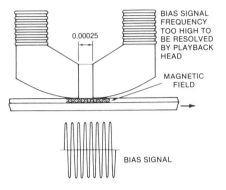

(A) Playback head gap.

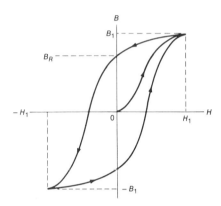

Fig. 1-12. The familiar *B-H* curve showing magnetization as a result of input signal.
(From Howard Tremaine, Audio Cyclopedia, *p. 808)*

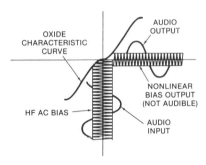

(B) Bias current applied with audio signal.

Fig. 1-13. Bias current is combined with audio signal.
(From Howard Tremaine, Audio Cyclopedia, *pp. 770-771)*

The selection of bias is usually controlled by a switch located on the front panel of the tape deck, and set according to the tape being recorded or played back.

Playing Back the Taped Audio Signal

After the tape is recorded it is rewound to the start of the recording, and the recorder is put into the play mode. In the record mode the record head was fed a signal. In playback the playback head will be used to recover the signal from the tape. As the tape passes in front of the head gap, the alignment of the particles on the tape will affect the flux across the head gap. These changing magnetic lines induce a voltage in the coils in the audio head. Since the alignment of the magnetic particles on the tape is proportional to the recorded signal, the induced

voltage during playback is also proportional to the recorded frequency.

After the Audio Signal Is Created

In either the case of the record disc or the audio tape recorder, after the audio signal has been converted into an electronic signal it must be amplified to a level that can drive a set of audio speakers. Low-level, or first-stage, amplification is usually done within the turntable or tape deck. Final, or high-level, amplification is usually done in a separate amplifier.

With the advent of higher-density audio tapes it was necessary to change the bias level in order to shift the recording point and to maintain a flat frequency response over a greater range of frequencies. Different types of tapes require different bias settings. Mismatching bias settings can have a great effect on the quality of the recorded signal. High bias can cause a loss of high-frequency response. Too little bias will distort the recording by overemphasizing high frequencies and distorting low frequencies.

For today's audio recorders, correct tape bias is a matter of matching the setting on the recorder with the type of tape used.

Playing Back the Tape

Just as bias ensures that the complete range of audio frequencies is recorded over a linear portion of the tape, *equalization* is the companion process that results in a flat playback response. Bias and equalization work hand in hand and must be set to match each other for good-quality signal playback.

During recording, the high frequencies of the audio signal are boosted in amplitude. This process is known as *preemphasis*. An example of preemphasis is shown in Fig. 1-14. The amount of preemphasis is dependent on the tape speed and tape formulation. Higher tape speeds can allow shorter preemphasis durations. This requires change in recording bias as well. While boosting the high frequencies helps in the recording process, it is not a true representation of the original audio signal, and therefore a reverse operation must be performed in playback. The playback process must deemphasize the signal at the rate it was preemphasized during recording. Slower than recorded deemphasis will leave some of the high-frequency spikes and accompanying noise in the playback signal. Faster than recorded deemphasis will roll off high frequencies which contain information. This will give the playback signal a basslike quality.

As matching biasing, preemphasis, and deemphasis are so critical to the reproduction of the audio signal, random settings of any one would result in noncompatibility between record-

ings made on one manufacturer's recorder and played back on another. To avoid this, the timing of preemphasis and deemphasis was agreed on among audio tape cassette manufacturers. For high-density audio tapes this figure is set at 70 microseconds. (A microsecond is one-millionth of a second.) For normal bias tapes playback equalization is 120 microseconds.

The differences between the biasing and equalization applied to normal and high-density tapes result in a difference in the amount of output signal noise. These differences can be heard by recording a tape with no signal input. The playback of such a recording would contain the noise created by the system electronics, which is known as *background noise* and sounds like a hiss. Normal-density tapes produce a higher hiss sound than high-density tapes.

AUDIO TAPE: THE FOUNDATION OF MAGNETIC RECORDING

As was previously described, magnetic energy is retained when an object's metal particles align in the same direction of the applied magnetic flux. The quantity, size, shape, and distance between the particles all play a part in determining the quality of the recorded signal. In an ideal situation the particles should be uniform. This allows for signal saturation in proportion to the applied flux. Particle shape accounts for high-frequency response. The greater the ratio of particle length to width, the better the magnetic performance and the better the overall frequency response. Of course, particle spacing is an important consideration. If a particle is not available to accept the incoming flux, the signal will not be recorded by that particle. A good-quality tape will contain tightly packed particles that take advantage of every bit of flux.

Fig. 1-14. A typical recording equalization curve. *(From Howard Tremaine,* Audio Cyclopedia, *p. 824)*

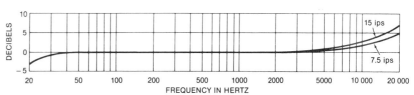

Finally, there is the consideration of the quality of the particle itself. Standard tapes, first developed in cassette in the 1960s, use an iron oxide compound. The 1970s found the introduction of chromium dioxide (CrO_2) tape. This was the first type of tape that allowed for higher bias/equalization settings, which gave greater signal performance and higher frequency response. The goal was to increase signal retention by increasing particle purity. The means was to create a pure metal tape. The problem was the instability of pure metal tape. While oxides increased tape stability, they introduced impurities that limited the quality of the recorded signal. Pure metal is subject to oxidation and the results are the same as a metal fence rusting due to weather. To prevent this, it was necessary to develop pure metal alloys that would resist oxidation. Metal tape became a reality in the late 1970s and along with it a new group of bias/ equalization settings and increased signal performance.

The signals we have been dealing with are recorded and reproduced in their analog state. This type of signal is a result of physical variables which are represented by an infinite number of numerical reference points. The problem that exists in analog signals is due to the components that are responsible for processing the signal. Resistors, capacitors, transistors, record discs, magnetic recording heads, and tapes all impede the reproduction of full fidelity audio signals. And the infinite signal levels lead to infinite possibilities of introducing noise into the signal.

The process of signal amplification is accomplished by passing audio signals through additional components. Thus signal amplification comes about at the cost of signal quality. In the next chapter we'll discuss the specifications that determine signal quality.

2
Problems of Audio Signal Processing

The methods of creating audio which were discussed in chapter 1 describe audio in terms of analog processing. This type of signal is expressed as a variable along the processing path. As a result of being a variable, subject to a variety of different signal levels and variations, the audio signal can also include a number of components not found in the original signal. Rather than add to the audio signal, these additional components detract from it. They occur due to abnormalities in the system creating or reproducing audio and are present in either the electronics that process the signal or the device that is responsible for transferring the signal to the medium.

In order to best understand the effects of distortion on signal transfer and processing, it is first necessary to understand the specifications of the performance of audio equipment.

FREQUENCY RESPONSE

Of all the specifications, *frequency response* serves as the primary specification by which products

are judged. Frequency response is the way in which different frequencies are affected by passing through the electronic components and wiring of a system. As previously described, audio electronic signals refer to a grouping of alternating current cycles. The frequency increases as the number of cycles that occur in the period of a second increases. Electronic circuits offer a certain resistance to signals passing through them.

Alternating current circuits (as opposed to direct current circuits) are in a constant state of change. These changes, created by the changing amplitude of the sine wave, build up magnetic fields, which in turn oppose any change in the current. For alternating current circuits, this opposition to changing current is known as *inductive reactance*. It is expressed by the formula

$$X_L = 2\pi f L$$

where

X_L = inductive reactance in ohms,
f = frequency of the signal in hertz,
L = inductance in henrys.

The henry (H) is the unit of inductance, which is the opposition to a change of current because of a magnetic field associated with the current.

Since the formula is linear, any increase in either the frequency or component inductance will increase the inductive reactance. Increases in circuit inductance result from the amount of processing the signal is subjected to. For any given circuit, however, we can assume that once the design is fixed, so will be the component inductance. Thus the major variation in the equation is frequency. As frequency increases, the faster buildup of the magnetic field results in a greater amount of inductive reactance. The greater the amount of inductive reactance, the greater is the loss of signal amplitude at high frequencies.

Audio reproduction devices attempt to reproduce signals across the entire range of audible frequencies of 20 to 20 000 hertz. The limitation of circuit inductive reactance prevents this and at some point the loss of signal amplitude will render it useless.

THE DECIBEL

The unit for measuring and comparing signal levels is known as the decibel (dB). Due to the characteristics of the human ear, every time we double the strength of a sound, we hear only a linear increase in sound. So as the intensity of the signal increases at a rate of 1:2:4:8:16:32, we hear a loudness increase of 1:2:3:4:5:6. These differences in signal strength and resulting sound as interpreted by our hearing show that sound could not be measured conveniently in terms of linear signal gains and losses. Consequently the decibel became the value at which our ears recognize a change in volume.

The decibel also became an important qualitative measure for signal amplitude. The power of a signal is represented by the formula $P = EI = I^2R = E^2/R$. Power can then be proportional to either the voltage squared or the current squared. As a result a loss of 30 percent of signal amplitude represents a 50-percent loss of power. Mathematically, $0.707 \times 0.707 = 0.5$.

As the decibel is based on logarithmic changes, the change of signal amplitude from 1 volt to 0.707 volt represents a loss of 3 decibels, which in turn yields the 50-percent loss of power. A reduction in signal amplitude which is less than 3 decibels is not generally considered objectionable by the average person. This relationship between signal loss and our hearing marks the -3-decibel level as the cutoff for measuring frequency response.

Measurements of frequency response are not limited only to losses. An increase of 3 decibels results in doubling the signal intensity.

The ideal frequency response of an audio system is flat, with no deviation in amplitude over the audible range of frequencies. The specification of frequency response is indicated by the range of frequencies where signal amplitude deviates no more than ±3 decibels from the signal amplitude at the lowest frequency, which is usually 20 or 25 hertz. Frequency response for an analog audio system would probably reach this point prior to the upper limit of the audible range. A typical specification for an audio cassette deck would be:

$$25\text{-}17\ 000\ \text{Hz},\ \pm 3\ \text{dB}.$$

Other specifications relate to frequency, in one way or another, by describing the amount of distortion introduced into the sine waves which compose the audio signal.

WOW AND FLUTTER

In any form of an electromechanical device there will be some form of instability. In either the case of the record turntable or the audio tape recorder, the fidelity of signal recording or reproduction is dependent on maintaining a constant speed of movement for the record or tape. Considering the record stylus or audio head as a given, changing the speed of the medium will change the frequency of the reproduced signal. Slowing down the speed of the record disc or tape will reduce the output frequency. Speeding up the record or tape will increase the output frequency. In either case any change from the proper speed of the equipment ($33^1/_3$ revolutions per minute for LP record discs and $1^7/_8$ inches per second (4.76 centimeters per second) for standard Philips audio cassettes will introduce new frequencies that were not present in the original signal.

These variations are known as wow and flutter. *Wow* is used to describe variations in frequency that occur due to electromechanical drive errors. The responsibility of maintaining a constant drive speed is dependent on the operation of the system's servo control circuit. In any servo system the object is to compare a variable to a fixed reference, and create an output as close to the fixed reference as possible. In audio record and tape systems the speed variation occurs due to the force applied to the drive motors. Left uncontrolled, the turntable drive and tape drive motors would turn at their maximum speed, depending on the voltage applied to them. The role of the servo system is to brake the speed of the motor to make the overall speed remain constant. Electromechanical servo systems are fairly accurate and, as a result, variations are kept to a minimum. Such variations below 5 hertz are defined as wow.

While drive motors are expected to yield some speed variations during the course of normal operation, record discs themselves and audio tape are not. Disc warping or anything that inhibits the ability of the tape to move will generate fluctuations with a repetition cycle on the order of 8 hertz or greater. As the frequency of these fluctuations becomes greater, the change in pitch is far more noticeable. These faster fluctuations are known as *flutter*.

Measuring Wow and Flutter

As previously noted, our ears discriminate changes in sound based on changes in intensity. A change from one frequency to another often occurs during the playback of an audio signal, particularly the playback of music. Under those circumstances the ear would interpret a change in frequency as normal. In interpreting wow and

flutter as a distortion, the change in frequency is accompanied by a change in intensity or signal power. The method for measuring wow and flutter is to measure changes in the amplitude of the output signal.

The unit used for this measurement is the *root mean square* or *rms* value. While direct current (dc) represents a measurable constant value at any given point, alternating current (ac) does not. It is constantly changing over the course of the sine wave. Since both voltage and current are factors of power, by squaring either and then taking the average, the value of how effective the ac will be in relationship to its peak can be found. The result is that an ac sine wave has an effective value of 0.707 of its peak value. At this point the ac sine wave will have the same effective value as dc. (A 100-volt ac supply will produce the same amount of light from a bulb as 70.7 volts of dc will.)

The term root mean square is also used to indicate the change of signal caused by the deviation of frequency. Typical readings from properly operating equipment would produce a change of less than 0.05 percent.

THE SIGNAL-TO-NOISE RATIO

At the point where audio signals are transferred from the stylus, or magnetic head, signal levels are low. In order to drive a speaker the signal must be processed by various stages of amplification. The resulting signal contains all the qualities of the signal from the source medium. This includes not only the signal information but also the noise contained within the signal. Every electronic signal contains some noise, which is present due to both the medium producing the signal and the internal circuits of the amplification system. For records, noise can occur due to geometric changes in the structure of stylus and the groove. When the stylus rides in a space not representing the original audio signal, variations result which produce a distorted output. An extreme example of this condition would be a scratched disc which would completely derail the stylus, causing it to skip over the information contained within the groove.

For audio tape the loss of tape oxide is the equivalent to a record scratch. The lack of oxide makes it impossible for any signal to be recorded or reproduced from the tape. Unlike the record stylus, the loss of information from the tape is localized to a specific area, and the head doesn't randomly skip to another section of the tape.

More often, the introduction of noise in the amplification system is not so extreme. Deviation in the medium will usually result in a hiss or rumbling sound. Noise is characteristically a function of a low-amplitude signal contained in a high frequency. The wider the frequency response, the greater is the potential for noise.

Differences in ground potential between the various components in the system can lead to a condition known as *hum*. While the existence of hiss and rumble requires that the signal medium be in contact with the pickup device, hum can be heard by turning up the volume with all the components on. In many cases how much the various forms of distortion detract from the quality of the audio signal is a matter of the listener's opinion.

Measuring the Signal-to-Noise Ratio

The signal-to-noise ratio is a ratio between signal information and noise content. Since the noise is an audio signal, it is measured in terms of its intensity. This makes the unit for measuring noise the same as that for measuring audio strength. In both cases the decibel is used. For every change of 3 decibels the intensity of the noise doubles in relationship to the signal. A decrease in the ratio of the signal to the noise means that the relative amount of noise contained in the audio signal has increased. The signal-to-noise ratio found at the internal point where the audio signal is produced is important for two reasons. First, each amplifier that processes the audio signal has its own noise factor, which adds to the noise, thereby decreasing the signal-to-noise ratio. A typical amplifier can have a noise factor of 3 to 6 decibels, resulting in an output signal which has two

to four times the noise content of the input signal. The greater the signal-to-noise ratio at the stylus or magnetic head is, the greater the resulting signal-to-noise ratio after the signal has been amplified. Second, the signal-to-noise ratio must be taken into consideration when copying tapes. Each tape copy will add more noise to the preceding generation. Distortion marginally acceptable in a first reproduction of an original recording can become objectionable in the playback of a copy. Typical signal-to-noise ratios for analog devices range from 60 to 70 decibels.

CHANNEL SEPARATION

In any stereo audio recording or reproduction device, the proximity of the left and right audio channels raises the possibility that the signals from one channel can intermix with the signals from the other. The crossover between the two channels can cause distortion and degrade the stereo image.

The greater the physical and electrical distance is between the two channels, the better the quality of the output sound. This specification is known as *channel separation*. It is an effect of the pickup device and the recording medium. Good channel separation depends on two factors. The first is the area needed to read and write the signal. For a given area, such as the size of a record groove or the width of the audio tape, the smaller the space required to accommodate the signal, the greater the remaining room on the medium to keep the channel signals separated. Second is the ability of the pickup device to read or track the individual channel signal. Like other methods of measuring audio performance, channel separation is measured in decibels. The higher the decibel value, the greater is the channel separation.

For record discs, mixing of track signals can occur due to worn or damaged grooves or stylus. For audio tape a recorder's poor separation can be the result of overdriven record current or misalignment of the playback head. In either case, poor channel separation is usually the result of a defect.

Specifications are used to judge the performance of equipment. An understanding of specifications is based on an understanding of the performance and problems of audio recording and reproduction equipment.

Regardless of the medium used to record or reproduce the signal, the definition of these specifications remains the same. As a result they can be used to compare the performance of one type of equipment to another. In later chapters we'll use specifications to compare the performance of analog reproduction equipment, such as the record disc and audio tape, with that of the digital compact disc.

3

Basic Digital Theory

In the previous chapter we touched on the structure of the analog signal. In electronics there are two basic electronic signals, analog and digital. Analog signals can exist in a variety of forms. They can be either alternating current (ac), changing in state from positive to negative, or direct current (dc), either positive or negative, steady state. In either case an analog signal has the characteristic of existing in a smooth or continuous form.

THE DIGITAL SIGNAL

While analog signals vary to a great degree, digital signals do not. Digital signals exist in a binary form, i.e., there are only two possible states. Fig. 3-1 shows the amplitude variations of typical analog and digital waveforms. The differences between analog and digital signals can be illustrated in the following manner. Turning on an audio amplifier is an action which can be considered digital, as the amplifier is in one of two states, either on or off. Once the amplifier is on, the volume can be varied over an infinite number of levels. The volume is continuous over

a wide range of levels. This represents an analog signal.

Digital signals are a series of pulses. Even with the restrictions on digital signals, they can be found in different forms. A digital signal can exist between zero and a positive potential, zero and a negative potential, and a positive and a negative potential.

The Development of Digital Signals

The use of digital signals increased with the growth of integrated circuits. These devices enabled signals to be processed in combinations of high and low states, and differences in signals could be detected based on the frequency of these changes. In the earliest form of digital technology the mechanical function keyboard controls of many consumer items were replaced with soft-touch, single-conductor cable remote and wireless infrared controls. Next, digital circuits were developed for controlling system servos as variations in tape and head speed (in the case of video recorders) could be accurately sampled and regulated. In its present state of development digital technology is used to create

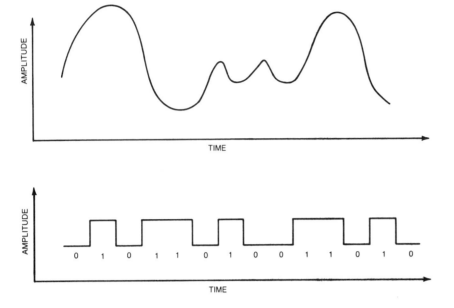

Fig. 3-1. Analog waveforms represent a wide range of amplitude levels. Digital waveforms represent just two. *(From Ken Pohlmann,* Principles of Digital Audio, *p. 28)*

and process audio and video signals. The compact audio disc player is unique in that it is one of the first consumer products that represents the utilizations of digital technology in all its forms for system and servo control, as well as for creating and processing the audio signal.

Advantages of Digital Signals

The advent of the digital signal usage came about due to the *ease of design*. The variables involved in analog circuit design require that a test design, known as a *breadboard*, be created to ensure its workability. Because analog circuits are subject to outside interference due to component usage and wiring, the layout of a test circuit is mandatory. The binary states of digital circuits help in rejecting many of these outside interferences. In addition, as the output can only be one of two states at any given instant, the predictability of digital circuit design is much greater than that of analog. As a result the time it takes to design, test, and place circuits using digital technology into production is shorter than that of analog. This makes digital circuits more cost-effective for product design and manufacturing.

The simplicity of using digital circuits yields three other important advantages over analog. The first is *stability*. The linear range of analog circuits makes them dependent on the stability of the components used. As these components are subject to environmental variations, such as temperature, the operation of the circuit can drift, making it unusable. This tendency of analog circuits to drift increases with manufacturing component imperfection and age. Digital circuits are only concerned with sensing the switching point that determines the transition between high to low (or low to high). Therefore the use of digital circuits eliminates interference and aging problems, but allows room for component changes. This makes digital circuits more *accurate* than analog. The output of an analog circuit will result in either a true or not-true condition based on the signal input. Outside signal rejection and stability result in greater accuracy. Finally, there is the range of *signal-handling capacity*. The range of signal levels that can be handled by digital signals is much greater than that of analog, which can become noisy and saturate at high signal amplitudes. This limits the dynamic range of analog circuits. But with digital technology any range of signal-handling capacity can be realized.

THE FUNDAMENTALS OF LOGIC

The advantages of digital circuits is their simplicity in operating in only one of two states, on or off. Since these states can be expressed as either a 1 or 0, digital circuits can be written in terms of mathematical equations. Combination of ones and zeros would yield predictable results. The type of math is a form of algebra. Digital equations are figured in terms of Boolean algebra, which is a deductive system of theorems using symbols to express AND, OR, and NOT propositions. This system is named after the famous English mathematician, George Boole (1815-1864), who developed it.

Boolean Symbols

Three of the symbols used in Boolean algebra equations are the plus sign ($+$), the multiplication sign ($\cdot$) and the equals sign ($=$). The variables in logic equations are usually expressed as an X and a Y. The functions are as follows.

The plus sign ($+$) is used to represent a logic OR function. This means that when either variable of the equation is positive the result will be positive. In the statement $X + Y = 1$, if either X or Y is positive, then the result will be positive.

The multiplication sign ($\cdot$) is used to represent the AND function. Both X and Y must be positive for the result to be positive. If X or Y is not logic 1, then mathematically it is impossible for the result to be anything else than logic 0.

The equals sign has the same meaning in Boolean algebra as in common algebraic equations. It separates the variables from the results. Each side of the equation must be balanced. For example, if X and Y have the same value, then reasoning says that $X = Y$.

We can use three types of digital variables to create a Boolean operation, the NOT function. This function is used to express the complement or inverse of a logic value. Since digital logic values are either positive or negative, then a value expressed as a 1 can only have an inverted value of 0. The complement carries a bar over it to indicate its value as zero, thus if $X = 1$, then $\overline{X} = 0$.

Logic Functions and Symbols

Electronic circuits do not use algebraic symbols to express equalities. Instead, signals are processed through components which alter the signal states between the input and output. These processing components are expressed by symbols which embody the functions of AND, OR, and NOT.

In the simplest form a logic equation can be expressed as an equality. The signal is transmitted on a continuous single piece of wire. The state of the polarity at input point A is the same at output point B. This type of logic equation usually represents a noninverting amplifier. In this case the output signal amplitude is greater than the input. In Fig. 3-2 the multiplication or AND function has two possible inputs, X and Y. The two inputs must be the same in order for an equivalent output. The function can be thought of as a series circuit having two switching points. For the output to be true each of the inputs must be true.

Like the AND function, the OR function in Fig. 3-2 has two possible inputs. Using the plus sign means that only one of the inputs has to be true in order for the output to be true. This function is represented by a parallel circuit, so the signal can take one path *or* the other in order to reach the output.

Variations on the Basics

The basic circuits just discussed can be combined into other simple but useful circuits, which have become standard logic building blocks.

The N Function—In each case the polarity of the normal output signal can be expressed in its opposite state by adding a small circle at the output. The OR and AND functions become NOT-OR and NOT-AND, better known as NOR and NAND. To find the output value for a NOR or NAND circuit,

COMPLEMENT $F = \bar{X}$

X	$\bar{X}$
0	1
1	0

AND $F = X \cdot Y$

X	Y	$X \cdot Y$
0	0	0
0	1	0
1	0	0
1	1	1

OR $F = X + Y$

X	Y	$X + Y$
0	0	0
0	1	1
1	0	1
1	1	1

EXCLUSIVE-OR
$F = X \oplus Y$

X	Y	$X \oplus Y$
0	0	0
0	1	1
1	0	1
1	1	0

NAND $F = \overline{X \cdot Y}$

X	Y	$\overline{X \cdot Y}$
0	0	1
0	1	1
1	0	1
1	1	0

NOR $F = \overline{X + Y}$

X	Y	$\overline{X + Y}$
0	0	1
0	1	0
1	0	0
1	1	0

Fig. 3-2. Boolean operators. *(From Ken Pohlmann,* Principles of Digital Audio, *p. 35)*

apply the same method for an OR or AND circuit and invert the output or conclusion. In the most basic form of the NOT function, a negative input would yield a positive output.

The Exclusive-OR Function––The exclusive-OR circuit functions in a manner similar to that of the standard OR circuit. The difference is that the exclusive-OR function takes into account the numerical value of the input bits. If the number of bits is even, the output will be 0. If the number of bits is odd, the output will be 1.

POSITIVE AND NEGATIVE LOGIC

In terms of their schematic values the differences between OR, AND, NOT, NOR and NAND can be expressed in terms of either positive or negative logic. When the logic 1 state is represented by a more positive voltage and the logic 0 state by the more negative voltage, the system is known as positive logic or positive-true logic. When the logic 1 state is represented by the more negative voltage, and the logic 0 state by the more positive voltage, the logic system is negative. As the use of one system instead of the other can change to the meaning of the output of the processing components, it is necessary to know which system is being used. Often people who draft circuits express negative logic by attaching a 0 to the input or output of the circuit.

BINARY NUMBER SYSTEMS: DIGITAL COUNTING

The system we normally use for counting is known as the *decimal* system. Numbers are arranged from 0 to 9 according to their weight by tens. For example, using the number 123, each of the numbers will take on a meaning as a multiple of ten depending on their position in the number. As a result 123 is 1×10^2 plus 2×10^1 plus 3×10^0. By using the decimal number system an infinite number of combinations can be created. In this way the decimal number system is similar to, and can be used for measuring, analog states.

Binary Numbers

In the decimal system the numbers 0 through 9 offer ten possibilities. Another name for this system is base 10. Binary digits (bits) have only two possible values, 1 or 0, and the binary system is sometimes referred to as the base 2 system. Each digit position in a binary number is weighted with a value equal to a multiple of 2. The first number position, when zero, is equal to 0×2^0. When it is 1, its value is equal to $1 \times 2^0 = 1$. The value of the total number is read from the right, which represents the least significant digit (LSD, the digit with the least weight), to the left side. The last digit on the left side carries the most weight and is known as the

HOWARD W. SAMS & COMPANY

ℋℋ

Bookmark

DEAR VALUED CUSTOMER:

Howard W. Sams & Company is dedicated to bringing you timely and authoritative books for your personal and professional library. Our goal is to provide you with excellent technical books written by the most qualified authors. You can assist us in this endeavor by checking the box next to your particular areas of interest.

We appreciate your comments and will use the information to provide you with a more comprehensive selection of titles.

Thank you,

Vice President, Book Publishing
Howard W. Sams & Company

COMPUTER TITLES:

Hardware
- ☐ Apple 140   ☐ Macintosh 101
- ☐ Commodore 110
- ☐ IBM & Compatibles 114

Business Applications
- ☐ Word Processing J01
- ☐ Data Base J04
- ☐ Spreadsheets J02

Operating Systems
- ☐ MS-DOS K05   ☐ OS/2 K10
- ☐ CP/M K01   ☐ UNIX K03

Programming Languages
- ☐ C L03   ☐ Pascal L05
- ☐ Prolog L12   ☐ Assembly L01
- ☐ BASIC L02   ☐ HyperTalk L14

Troubleshooting & Repair
- ☐ Computers S05
- ☐ Peripherals S10

Other
- ☐ Communications/Networking M03
- ☐ AI/Expert Systems T18

ELECTRONICS TITLES:

- ☐ Amateur Radio T01
- ☐ Audio T03
- ☐ Basic Electronics T20
- ☐ Basic Electricity T21
- ☐ Electronics Design T12
- ☐ Electronics Projects T04
- ☐ Satellites T09

- ☐ Instrumentation T05
- ☐ Digital Electronics T11

Troubleshooting & Repair
- ☐ Audio S11   ☐ Television S04
- ☐ VCR S01   ☐ Compact Disc S02
- ☐ Automotive S06
- ☐ Microwave Oven S03

Other interests or comments: _____

_____

_____

Name_____

Title _____

Company _____

Address _____

City _____

State/Zip _____

Daytime Telephone No. _____

A Division of Macmillan, Inc.
4300 West 62nd Street
Indianapolis, Indiana 46268

22521

Bookmark

HOWARD W. SAMS
& COMPANY

most significant digit (MSD). The weight of each position increases by doubling the weight value from the position to its immediate right. For example, in the binary number 1111 the first four positions are as follows:

$$(1 \times 2^3) + (1 \times 2^2) + (1 \times 2^1) + (1 \times 2^0)$$
$$8 \qquad 4 \qquad 2 \qquad 1$$

Therefore the binary number 1111 equals 8 + 4 + 2 + 1 = 15.

The binary system offers advantages over the decimal system due to the number of digits (two) that the system has to deal with. This makes the binary numbers better for use in designing computer and other electronic systems that need to handle large numbers.

THE DIGITAL PROCESS: CONVERTING THE SIGNAL

Digital audio begins as an analog signal. The processing of audio for a compact disc system requires that the input audio signal be converted into a digital signal, recorded on the disc, processed as a digital signal, and finally returned to its analog form in order to be heard through a speaker.

The Analog-to-Digital Process

In analog audio the signal processing deals with the entire signal. The output requires that the entire signal be present. Components can add distortion and noise to the signal. These distortions can be passed on to amplification stages and appear at the speaker. For analog-to-digital conversion the audio signal is first sampled at a fast rate, as shown in Fig. 3-3C. This action can be accurately described as a sample and hold process. The audio signal is first processed and stored by analog means. This can be as simple as amplifying the signal and allowing the voltage to build up in a capacitor. An internal clock provides the pulses that sample the signal. At each sample point the signal charge on the

capacitor is cut off and read out into the system. The state of the signal is held until the next clocking pulse. Fig. 3-4 shows the process. This presents a possible problem. If the sampling rate is too low, fast-rate analog voltage swings can be missed and the details of the audio signal can be lost. While high-frequency sampling provides better signal resolution, it requires using more expensive components that result in higher product costs. Testing has shown that the sampling rate must be at least two times the highest system frequency. Since the highest frequency of the audible range is 20 kilohertz, the least acceptable sampling rate would be 40 kilohertz. As frequency processing must take into account some signal loss, a sampling frequency of 44.1 kilohertz is used.

Even with a sampling frequency as high as 44.1 kilohertz, problems can exist between it and the audio frequency. This occurs if any energy in the high end of the audio-frequency spectrum is allowed to mix with the sampling frequency. The resulting signal is amplified and, if left unchecked, could produce noise. To avoid this, the analog signal is limited by filtering to an upper limit of 20 kilohertz.

Successive Approximation

There are two important factors that must be taken into consideration when sampling the audio signal. The first is the rate at which the signal is sampled. The second is that the sampling include the complete range of audio frequencies from the lowest to the highest. Just randomly sampling the audio signal voltage would be an extremely slow process. An 8-bit system would require a sampling process involving 2^8, or 256, steps. The slowness of the process could mean that some of the range of audio signals is lost. This would result in a smaller than normal range of audio frequencies. Such distortion results in a loss of dynamic range.

The analog-to-digital conversion process speeds up signal sampling by making certain assumptions. By weighing two input variables, an assumption can be made as to the approximate voltage. The method of calculating the voltage

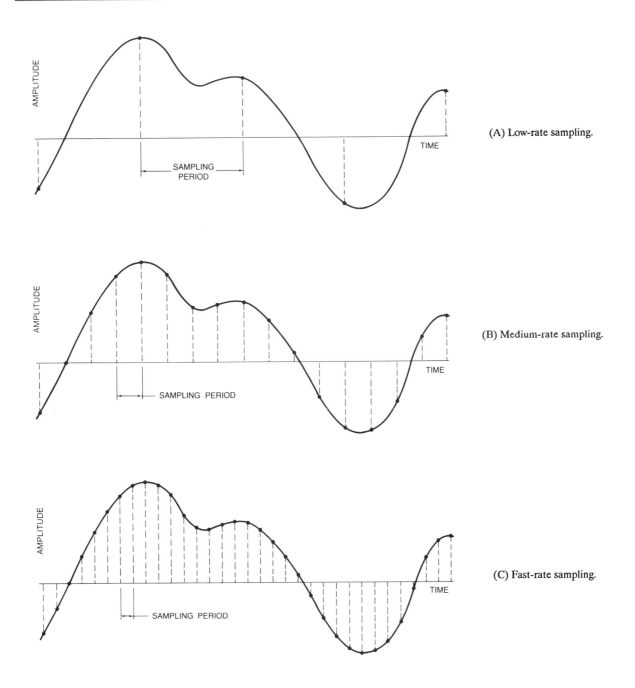

(A) Low-rate sampling.

(B) Medium-rate sampling.

(C) Fast-rate sampling.

Fig. 3-3. Sampling an audio analog waveform at various rates. *(From Ken Pohlmann,* Principles of Digital Audio, *p. 39)*

yields the name for the technique: successive approximation. By using this technique, the 2^8 steps required for sampling can be reduced to 8.

In the successive approximation process the audio voltage is fed into one input of an analog comparator. The comparator output is converted to a digital signal and compared to a preassigned, or reference, voltage, which is used to set the system's maximum voltage which can be digitized. First, the most significant bit is assigned a value of 1, while the remaining seven bits are set to zero. At this point the value of the digital word will be one-half of the reference voltage. If the audio input is higher than this level, the MSB is kept at the value 1. If it is less, the MSB is set to 0. The value of the MSB is stored. Then, the next

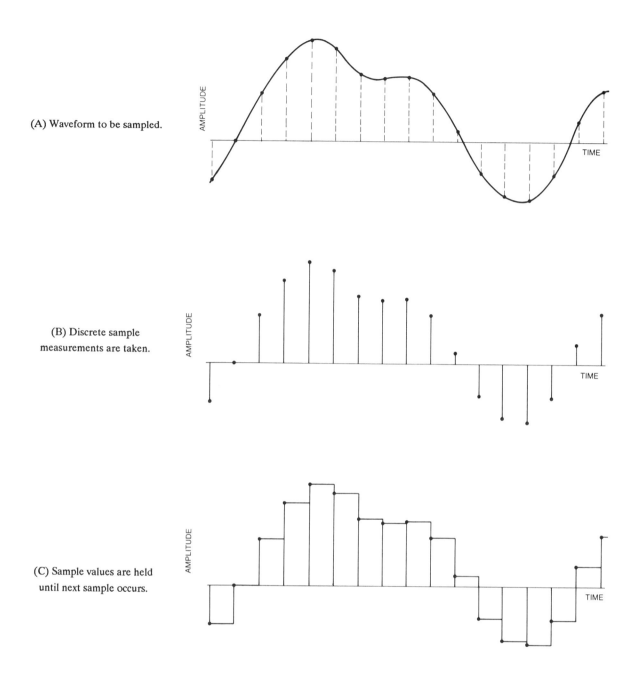

(A) Waveform to be sampled.

(B) Discrete sample measurements are taken.

(C) Sample values are held until next sample occurs.

Fig. 3-4. Sample and hold action. *(From Ken Pohlmann,* Principles of Digital Audio, *p. 41)*

highest significant bit is set to 1, while the remaining six bits are set to 0. Again the audio signal is compared with this new digital word. If the audio signal is higher, this bit is kept at 1; if the audio signal is lower, this bit is set to 0. The process repeats six more times for the remaining six bits. After all eight comparisons are done, the digital word will be that value which is closest to the value of the audio signal. This system will produce erroneous results, however, if the audio signal is allowed to go higher in voltage than the reference.

Example of a Successive Approximation with Four Samplings—Let's assume that an analog input with an unknown voltage of X is being processed by a processor performing four successive approximations. In the first approximation stage the voltage is compared with the highest bit value in the system. In a 4-bit system, the highest, or most significant bit (MSB) would be equal to 8. If the input voltage is greater than 8, the number is held or set. A set value is assigned a value of 1. During the next approximation stage, the bit to the right of the MSB is tested. The result is 8 + 4 = 12. For our example let's assume that this value is greater than the analog input voltage. As the 4 added to the 8 created a value greater than the input, the position representing the 4 is reset and takes on a value of 0. Next the value 2 position is tested and added to the 8. As this value is less than X, this bit is set and assigned a 1. Finally, the least significant digit is tested and added to the combination of 8 + 2. Previous to this approximation stage we determined that the combination of 8 + 4 (or 12) was greater than X, and the combination of 8 + 2 (or 10) was less than X. This means that the fourth sampled bit added to the 8 and 2 will result in 8 + 2 + 1 (or 11). As this value is equal to X, it is retained (set) and assigned a value of 1. The result is 1011, or the decimal number of 11. Instead of the analog-to-digital process requiring the time to perform 16 (or 2^4) samplings, the same result is realized in the time it takes to do just 4 samplings.

QUANTIZATION NOISE

As previously noted, the analog signal can have an infinite number of levels. Compared to successive approximation, analog processing is subject to a greater amount of sampling than digital. The error created by the infinitesimal variances of the analog signal and the fixed states of the digital signal create properties that were not present in the original analog input. These signal properties result in noise, which is known as *quantization noise*.

There are a number of possible methods for reducing quantization noise. One method is by increasing the sampling rate. Once again the problems of costs associated with higher-rate processing circuits come into consideration. A more often used method is to take advantage of the fixed properties of digital circuits to calculate the amount of noise introduced by a particular sampling rate. This value, known as a *dither*, is often added to the audio signal prior to quantization, in systems that require the highest accuracy.

ENCODING

Encoding is the process of arranging information into a specific pattern. In digital applications it can be considered to be a method for distinguishing when a particular bit is being sent. For example, are the bits sent MSB to LSB, or vice versa?

Encoding serves two major functions in the compact disc system. The first is to provide information other than audio. The second is to set the order of these various signals so that the industry can maintain interchangeability between various manufacturers of audio disc and compact disc players.

In itself, the process of converting an analog audio signal to digital numbers is very limited. The system only goes as far to ensure that a voltage level will be assigned a digital number. During the playback process a compact disc must be able to properly determine the speed of disc rotation as well as locate the selected audio track. These processes are accomplished by additional data bits included along with the digitized audio signal. These groups of bits must be positioned in uniform order so that the decoding system can recognize the differences between the audio and nonaudio data bits.

DIGITAL-TO-ANALOG CONVERSION

Digital-to-analog conversion represents the final stage of processing. For audio to be heard through a speaker system it must be in analog form.

The complexities of digital circuitry are reduced to the simplicity of $E = IR$, which defines different voltage levels by the changes of current through a resistor.

During the analog-to-digital process we used the positioning of ones and zeros to determine the value of the individual digit. The binary number 11111111 is the equivalent of decimal 255. However, the MSB 1 carries the value of 128, while the LSB 1 carries a weight of only 1. Thus the differences between larger and smaller voltages can be determined if a resistance network can be constructed that recognizes the weight of each digit based on its position. One such network is called a *resistive ladder*. A resistive ladder in a digital-to-analog converter is shown in Fig. 3-5. This circuit samples the digital

word and creates an output voltage by summing the values of all the individual digits. During the recording process each set of digits, or digital word, carries its own unique value taken from the input audio. As a result each individual word can be used to produce any of the infinite audio levels.

With one exception, the audio signal found at the resistive summing point is then amplified and buffered through conventional methods prior to reaching the speaker. In converting audio signals from digital to analog we must take into consideration the 44.1-kilohertz signal used as the sampling frequency. The conversion process requires additional complex filtering to ensure that the sampling frequency is not intermixed with the audio signal.

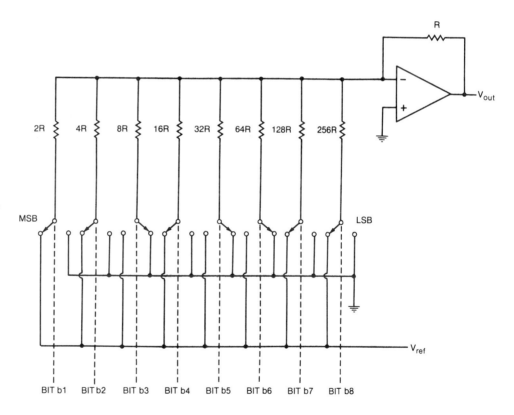

Fig. 3-5. Digital-to-analog converter containing a resistive ladder. *(From Ken Pohlmann,* Principles of Digital Audio, *p. 104)*

4

The Construction
of the CD Signal

In this chapter we will examine the various processes employed to generate the data stream which is recorded on a CD. It is not a simple matter of taking the digital signal from the A/D converter and laser cutting it onto the disc. The developers of the CD system took into consideration the all-important aspect of cost to the consumer. Certain processes, such as the cross-interleave Reed-Solomon code, and EFM, are employed to keep the yield of CD manufacturing high, and the cost of the playback optics low. And beyond this, the information is "grouped" before it is recorded. Actual "frames" of information are arranged before recording. Such strict organization allows for proper decoding of not only the digital audio signal but also the "extra" information, such as the time display information. But first, we'll start by looking at simple modulation systems.

THE MODULATION SYSTEM

The bandwidth of analog audio signals allows them to be recorded directly on the medium without change of their original form. The limitations of the signal processing system contribute to the inability of analog systems to reproduce signals approaching 20 kilohertz with high signal-to-noise ratios. Signal modulation is the process of changing or varying the signal so that it varies in step with the instantaneous value of another wave. It is used to aid in the reproduction of the high-frequency signal components. Often this process is used in video, where the signal is frequency modulated (fm).

In the application of digital signals we must take into account additional bandwidth over and above that contained in the original audio signal. This is used to digitally process the audio as well as record associated coding information. In analog processing, an ideal frequency response for both processing and recording medium would be that up to 20 kilohertz. Digital processing at sampling rate of 44.1 kilohertz requires a response 2.21 times that of 20 kilohertz. As an individual channel is processed into a 16-bit word, 44.1 kilohertz is multiplied by 16 bits per sample. This yields 705.6 kilobits per second. But this represents only audio data. The extra data bits such as the time and number of each selection, length of the disc, and synchronizing bits add to this figure to produce a total bit rate of 4.321 megabits per second. In order to reproduce the full audio bandwidth with a high signal-to-noise ratio and low distortion along with the other nonaudio bits, the CD system must subject the analog audio to a process of modulation. For CD systems the modulation process is the heart of the encoding system that transfers analog audio to the digital pulse train that becomes the signal impressed on the disc. This is actually a combination of various signal processes.

PULSE-CODE MODULATION

Pulse-code modulation, or PCM, is sometimes thought of as the complete conversion process that results in disc-ready data. In reality, PCM is only the beginning of the process. It is actually the system that converts analog signal waveforms to a series of binary pulses. It is composed of signal sampling, quantization, and coding. These processes were previously described in chapter 2. For compact disc systems, signal processing begins by sampling the analog input at the 44.1-kilohertz rate. The signal analog-to-digital conversion is only part of the process. Since the signal from both channels is read out by one pickup device, A/D conversion is required for each channel, both left and right. Each channel must be multiplexed prior to the final stage of modulation, as shown in Fig. 4-1. In addition to processing audio signals, other information pertaining to random track selection and information display are added to the audio signal. The ability to handle high-frequency, low-distortion signals along with associated signal information is the responsibility of the modulation system.

EIGHT- TO FOURTEEN-BIT MODULATION

In CD, the special modulation system is known as eight- to fourteen-bit modulation (EFM). Eight-

to fourteen-bit modulation is really more of a substitution process than a modulation process. This process substitutes 14-bit words for an incoming 8-bit word. This action allows for less rapid transitions and therefore effectively lowers the frequency of the data stream going onto the disc. In CD it had been decided the data stream on the disc shall not have fewer than 2 zeros between ones and no more than 10 zeros between ones (called the two-to-ten rule). This rule sets the frequency range of the data stream. The example in Fig. 4-2A shows an 8-bit word with rapid transitions, and Fig. 4-2B shows a corresponding 14-bit word which follows the two-to-ten rule. The fundamental reason for doing this is to limit the high-frequency content of the data stream, thereby allowing the use of less costly optics. It also maintains a minimum frequency required by the tracking and PLL circuits (which we'll encounter in chapter 8). EFM works in conjunction with a digital error-correction process known as the cross-interleave Reed-Solomon code (CIRC). During encoding error-correction precedes EFM.

The result of sampling the analog signal is a 16-bit word that represents the state of the analog signal at that one period. These words are grouped into frames, which occur at a rate of 7.35 kilohertz or a period of 136 microseconds. Each frame is marked by a synchronization symbol which is detected by the error-correction system so that the start of a new frame can be clearly found. Each audio sample is divided into symbols. A symbol is formed by splitting the 16-bit audio sample into two 8-bit symbols. It is these symbols which undergo EFM. This results in 24 audio symbols per frame.

ERROR CORRECTION

Although handling digital audio signals is designed to eliminate signal-processing errors, the transfer of the data stream to the surface of the master disc is still dependent on the physical relationship between the writing element and disc surface. The dependence of the signal

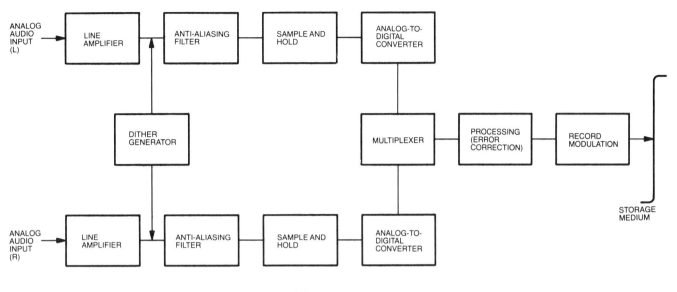

(A) Recording section.

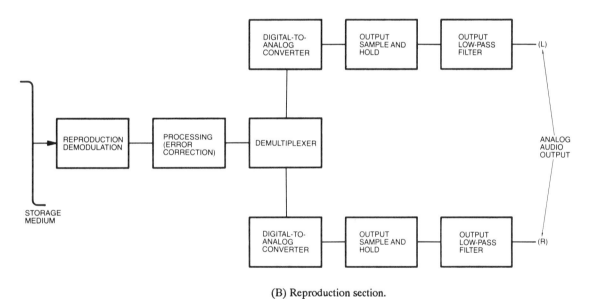

(B) Reproduction section.

Fig. 4-1. Block diagram of a PCM digitization system. Notice that the two inputs (stereo) are multiplexed to become just one channel. *(From Ken Pohlmann,* Principles of Digital Audio, *p. 119)*

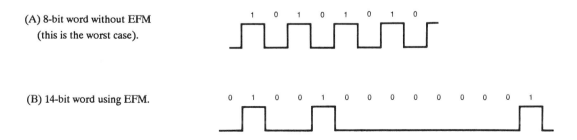

Fig. 4-2. EFM reduces the number of transitions.

transfer on an electromechanical device within a physical environment can result in data errors due to the following:

1. Even under highly controlled environmental conditions dust, fingerprints, and scratches can block or distort the transfer of a bit. This is particularly true when tape is used to accept the digitally processed signal, and the loss of tape oxide can contribute to additional signal loss.

2. Electromechanical variations result in a loss of consistency in the writing of the digital data and data bit distortions. These variations can take the form of servo loss or lack, and, in the case of magnetic tape, of tape-to-head contact.

Left uncorrected, data writing distortion would result in changes in the audio level of the reproduced signal, jitter, wow and flutter, and noise. Without a system to either overlook or correct distortions that occur in the writing process, the playback of digitally processed audio signals would offer quality little better than that of analog recording and playback.

TYPES OF DIGITAL WRITING ERRORS

Digitally processed signals can be subject to two types of errors. The first type is an individual bit error that has no relationship to other bit errors. It derives its name of "random error" by occurring at a random rate. The second type occurs when an error extends over a group of bits. It is called a *burst error*. Such errors can extend over the length of a word.

As important as error correction is to the reproduction of digital audio, it cannot be accomplished at the expense of the audio signal itself. The space of the disc does have its limitations, and any allocation of space for error-correcting information must be subtracted from the real estate otherwise available for the audio signal. To this end, every attempt must be made to maintain a low ratio of error correcting to audio.

There are two goals of error correction. First is to prevent these errors from occurring, and, second, when they occur, to make them more manageable by reducing their duration.

Correcting Short-Duration Random Errors

Short-term distortions can occur during the PCM or signal modulation process when a different binary state is received from the one sent. To prevent this, parity words made of 8 bits are added to the 24 audio symbols. A parity bit is an additional bit that is added to the information bits. The system is keyed to the number of ones required to re-create a number. It can be used to either reflect an odd- or even-parity state. For example, the number 9 written in binary form is 1001. For an odd-parity system an extra parity bit of 1 would be added to create an odd number of ones. The number 9 is now written in the following manner: 1001 1, where 1001 is the signal information, and the remaining 1 is the parity bit. In the event that a processing or transmission error causes the reception of an incorrect bit, the parity bit can be used to approximate the original state of the bit. Since the parity bit results from the signal information it is actually a product of its components. If we label the binary digits of the number 9 as A, B, C, and D, then the state of P would equal $A + B + C + D$. If during reproduction the A bit was not correctly received, it would be flagged by the parity bit and the equation $A = P - B - C - D$. In the CD system this type of parity system is referred to as a P parity. If the correction system depended solely on the use of a P parity check, it would be difficult if not impossible to correct for errors occurring in more than one component digit. A second kind of parity check system used in the CD system is called Q parity. The term Q is also a resultant of $A + B + C + D$, and the P parity. It, however, confirms its value by multiplying each of the component digits by a known constant. The use of both P and Q parity checks help to reduce multiple-bit errors occurring within an 8-bit audio symbol.

Correcting Long-Duration Burst Errors

As we can see from the example of parity errors, the longer the duration of the error, the harder it is to correct. The use of parity bits is limited in the duration of errors that can be corrected. Long-duration error conditions, particularly those caused by the environment, can extend over the range of several frames. When this occurs we must use a method known as *interleaving*.

In this recording process the order of the data is rearranged and no longer reflects a progressive count of 1, 2, 3, 4, 5, etc. When a burst error occurs, the distortion can affect a group of as large as several frames. By interleaving the signal we change the progressive order of the bits, as shown in Fig. 4-3. The result isolates the error groupings into individual bits. Now the individual error bit can be handled in the same manner as a random error, by using the parity bit check system. During playback the signal is deinterleaved so that the signals are reconstructed to their original form.

In the CD system there are actually two different interleaving actions performed. Interleaving is sometimes referred to as *scrambling*. The two stages of scrambling are referred to as C1 and C2. More simply stated, the C1 scrambling stage is a minor interleaving stage performed just before the P parity words. After this, the C2 scrambling stage is performed and then the Q parity words are derived. The C1 stage is usually considered to encompass both the minor interleaving and P parity processes. Similarly, the C2 stage is considered to be both the major interleaving and the Q parity processes (see Fig. 4-4).

Limitations of Error-Correcting Systems

Any type of system will have some limitations. In compact disc systems, error-correcting limitations exist in two forms: errors that are detected but cannot be corrected, and errors that are miscorrected. In reality, the function of digital disc error correction is not correction but concealment of random and burst errors. This is exactly the way the parity-bit check system works. By calculating the bit error from the parity check bit that represents the bit, some correction is achieved through bit concealment. Since disc space is at a premium, the generation of parity bits must be kept to the minimum required to do the job. With the use of more parity bits the probability of generating miscorrected bits would decrease, along with available audio disc space. Not enough error bits would result in too many uncorrected errors.

The method used to determine the correct placement of parity check bits is known as *distancing*. The process is governed by a code known as a Hamming code. Used in this capacity it is sometimes referred to as the Hamming distance. It measures the number of positions between two words having different bits. Hamming codes are not unique to compact disc systems. For example, a 4-bit word can be compared with 3 parity bits. The parity bits are then combined with the data bits for all the possible data bit combinations. In the compact disc, parity bits are added to check the contents of each grouping of 8-bit symbols. Combined with the interleaving process, the actual mechanism for checking errors occurs during playback when the signal is deinterleaved.

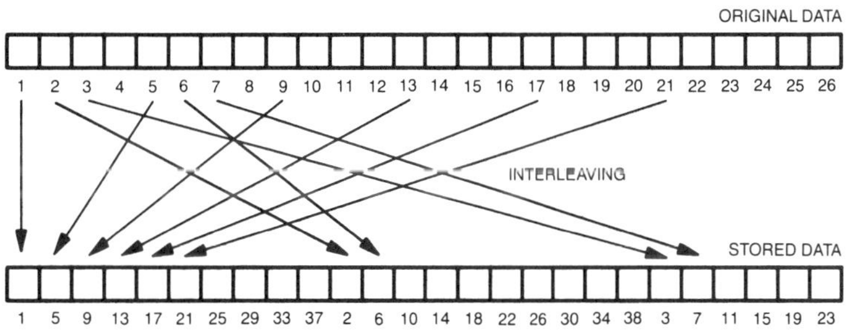

Fig. 4-3. An example of interleaving. *(From Ken Pohlmann,* Principles of Digital Audio, *p. 91)*

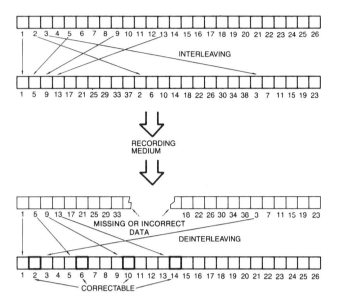

Fig. 4-4. Interleave and deinterleave process.
(From Ken Pohlmann, Principles of Digital Audio, *p. 99)*

CROSS-INTERLEAVE REED-SOLOMON CODE

The process of adding parity check codes and interleaving the signal is referred to as cross-interleave Reed-Solomon code, or CIRC. Interleaving the signal for dispersement of burst errors has previously been described. Reed-Solomon is the code applied to the interleaving process. The complexity of the code is of little importance for understanding how to troubleshoot the compact disc system. The code is contained within a large-scale integrated circuit fed by a random-access memory. Troubleshooting is relegated to the presence of voltage, ground, and pulse outputs.

CIRC is not restricted to solely an encoding process. Deinterleaving requires the application of additional Reed-Solomon codes to decode the audio signal back to its original structure. Decoding is accomplished by two separate linear Reed-Solomon code systems, C1 and C2. Signal flow through the decoder is from C1 to C2. The primary function of one of the decoders is to detect long-duration burst errors and to correct short-duration random errors. Its high rate of

detection capability enables the decoder to set up flags which then signal the second decoder, which corrects the burst errors and any random errors not corrected by the first decoder. A block diagram of the CIRC process is shown in Fig. 4-5.

COMBINING CIRC AND EFM

The error-correcting capability of the CIRC system is designed to match the 8-bit output of the PCM conversion process. Remember that if this signal were directly transferred onto the disc, a high probability would exist that transitions between 1, 0, 1, etc., are located adjacent to each other. If this occurs, the pickup system would have trouble distinguishing the differences in these bit patterns. The result would be a distorted playback. Distance becomes a key factor in helping the system to accurately read the differences between bits.

For compact disc systems the distance between bits takes two forms. The application of distance is used to correct the physical limitation of the pickup beam. Information bits impressed on the disc medium take the form of pits (indentures) and flats (no pits). If the flats or pits are located too close together, the pickup beam has problems in determining where the transition between the pit and flat occurs. Recall that this is why EFM is used. A one occurs on the transition between a pit and flat, and also on the fall between a flat and pit. This is shown in Fig. 4-6. This system is referred to as nonreturn-to-zero (nrz). The system is required to resolve the transition point. Pits positioned too close together can result in signals going unread. Flats located too close raise the possibility of the laser beam interpreting them as one long flat, and overlooking the pit. Because some of this signal information is used to control the speed of the motor, lost control information can result in an off-speed motor and lost audio content. To prevent this, the compact disc system, through EFM, has established a minimum and maximum transition length between pits and flats. This transition length is expressed in terms of bits and is set at a minimum of three bits (T_{min}, which is 2 zeros followed by a one) and a maximum of 11 bits (T_{max}, which is 10 zeros followed by a one).

When this resulting signal is used to cut the disc medium, the result is longer pits and flats, thus simplifying the player.

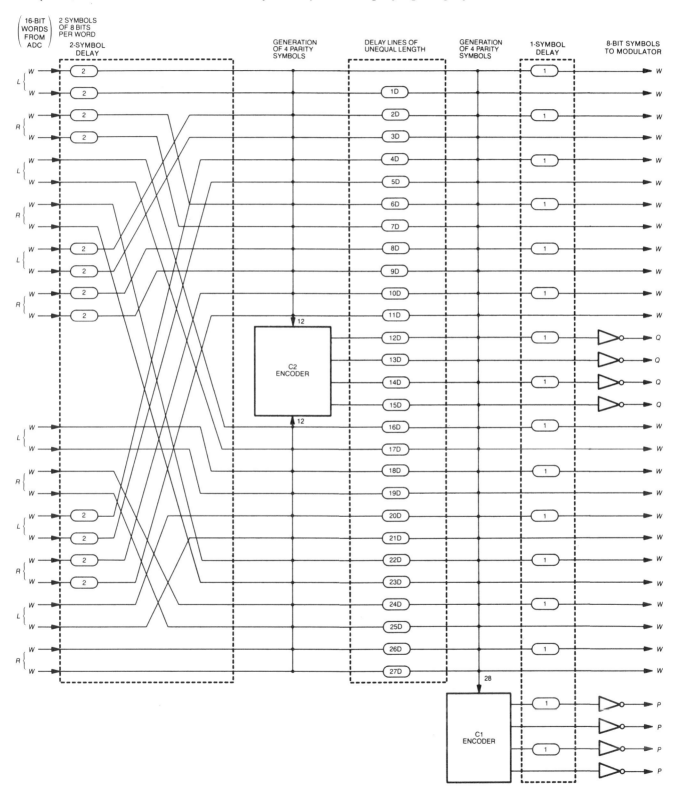

Fig. 4-5. CIRC encoding. *(From Ken Pohlmann,* Principles of Digital Audio, *pp. 226-227)*

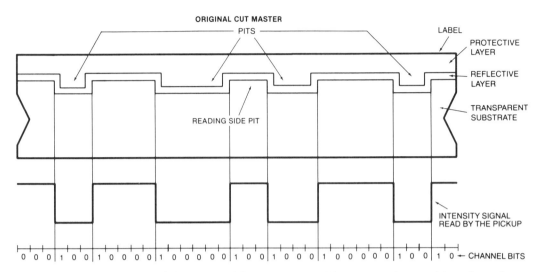

Fig. 4-6. Transitions between pit bottom and flat represent a binary 1; as do transitions from flat to pit.
(From Ken Pohlmann, Principles of Digital Audio, *p. 222)*

The distancing required by compact disc must be maintained during symbol transitions. The 8-bit code is the minimum required to contain the information of one symbol. As this information is in binary form the total possible combinations are 2^8, or 256. To stay within the confines of the two-to-ten rule of eight- to fourteen-bit modulation, or EFM, we find that using 8-bit data words is inadequate. An 8-bit word can have 256 different combinations of ones and zeros, but only about 100 of them satisfy the two-to-ten rule. In order to have at least 256 combinations which satisfy the rule, the use of 14-bit words is necessary. There are over 16 000 combinations of ones and zeros in a 14-bit word, and 267 of them satisfy the two-to-ten rule. This is why 8-bit words are replaced by 14-bit words.

MERGING BITS

After the EFM process, there are a series of 14-bit words, each following the two-to-ten rule. However, when placed on the disc, these 14-bit words will be arranged in succession, in serial form. When symbols are merged, the two-to-ten rule must continue to be satisfied. On merging, if the minimum distance requirement is not met, a 0 is issued. If the distance is too long, a 1 is

issued. By detecting the distance as too short or too long and issuing the closest bit value, the two-to-ten requirement is satisfied without introducing signal distortion. Three bits are used for merging, because they themselves can act as a T_{min} element (2 zeros followed by a one). In the worst case, where adjacent 14-bit words contain a long string of zeros, the insertion of a T_{min} element may be necessary. The longest stretch of zeros allowable is ten. A back-to-back sequence of 10 zeros followed by a one is found in CD, and is reserved for the synchronization word to be described later. It is important that such a long stretch of zeros not occur anywhere else (and certainly none longer than 10 zeros). If this were allowed, the lengths of the pits and flats would become longer, and the low-frequency content of the data stream would drop even lower. The operation of the playback tracking circuits and data recovery circuits (PLL) relies on constantly changing data, not data with very long sequences of zeros. If the tracking circuits do not see some kind of changing data, they may drift. Additionally, all analog-to-digital operations and encoding are done according to a master 4.321-megahertz clock. This clock is *not* recorded on the compact disc. The PLL circuit relies on constantly varying data in order to reconstruct the playback clock. Therefore the ability of the merging bits to raise the lowest recorded frequency is essential.

SYNCHRONIZING THE FRAME

After the EFM process it is necessary for the compact disc system to identify the start of each frame. The synchronizing frame signal is positioned at the head of each frame. During decoding, the start of frame must be identified in order to separate the data bits accurately. This process is similar to that of control pulses in a video tape recorder used to guarantee signal recovery, or the sync pulses of a television set used for picture stability, and, as in the case of video tape or television, without proper decoding of the frame sync pulse the rest of the information in the frame could not be properly decoded.

Processing audio data information alone is not enough to allow the compact disc system to reproduce audio properly. Recovery of the audio signal requires a constant electromechanical relationship between the pickup device and the disc medium. The data of each frame is placed on the disc in the same manner with a constant timing relationship. If the speed of the playback disc varied, it would make data recovery nearly impossible. As part of the signal mixing process a synchronizing signal is added to the EFM signal. The synchronization pattern consists of 24 channel bits which are connected to the rest of the bit pattern by three merging bits, as shown in Fig. 4-7.

CONTROL CHANNELS

While audio signals on the compact disc would not exist without audio data, and proper tracking of audio signals would not be possible without some sort of sync information, control channel

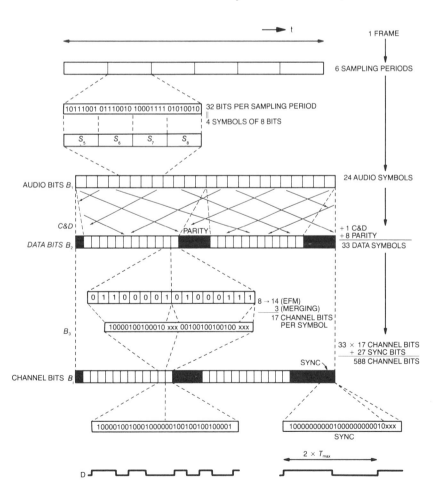

Fig. 4-7. Bit streams in the encoding system. *(Courtesy Philips. From Ken Pohlmann, Principles of Digital Audio, p. 229)*

information is not a fixed requirement of the system. The term control information may be a little bit misleading. The information contained within these codes is data which permits random access control and user display readouts. Control data code information is carried on a grouping of subcode channels labeled P to W. One complete unit of subcode information, called a *block*, is carried over a distance of 98 frames and occurs throughout the entire program. Since the duration of one frame is 136 microseconds, the duration of time required to read one subcode block information from all 98 frames is 13.3 milliseconds. Of the eight available subcode channels, only two, P and Q, are currently in use.

The P Channel

Within the P channel code there are two indication bits, called S0 and S1. These and the first two bits within any of the subcode channels are a part of the "block sync" word. This is not, however, to be confused with frame sync. The block sync word identifies which frame, in a group of 98 frames, contains the beginning of the subcode block. Subcode block sync performs the same basic duties as the frame sync—that of marking the beginning of a particular string of data. If a player started to decode the subcode block at some random point, the recovered subcode information would be meaningless. The P subcode is used to tell the system when the optics are in the middle of selection, as well as when the system is between music selections. It is also used after the lead in, which is prior to the start of the music, and prior to the lead out, which occurs when the last selection on the disc is playing. These such indications occur when the P channel goes from a low to a high state. When the P channel goes high, the P channel "flag" is said to have occurred.

The P channel flag has a minimum duration of 2 seconds, depending on the pause length. The term "pause" identifies the silent area between two tracks. If the pause length is greater than 2 seconds, the P channel flag will equal the duration of the pause. During the lead-in section of the disc (that area before the first selection) channel P is encoded in the same manner as is done for the musical portions. At the end of the lead-in section the P channel takes the form of the start flag for 2 to 3 seconds. During the last music track and prior to the lead out the P channel start flag is again issued for 2 to 3 seconds. The end of this flag signals the start of the lead out (or very end of the disc), during which the state of the P channel is 0. At the end of the lead out the P channnel switches between 0 and 1 at a frequency of 2 hertz.

The Q Channel

The key word used to describe the Q channel is information. The Q channel has two functions. In the first the Q channel provides information to the internal working of the playback compact disc. In the second it provides user information, often in the form of a front-panel display. These two information modes can be further divided. The internal information section consists of three blocks known as *control, address*, and *CRC*. The control group contains information on player functions, such as the number of recorded audio channels (the compact disc can have either two or four), whether preemphasis is used, and if digital copying of the disc is allowed. The CRC, cyclic redundancy check, is a 16-bit program added to data information in order to detect errors. The program selects a special number which is divided into the data. The same number is used in the encoding (recording) and decoding (playback) process. If no errors are present, the result of the division is 0; if errors are present, the result is 1. The CRC is used to detect errors for the Q data functions. The address code informs the systems of the correct Data Q mode.

Data Q is the second major operational Q mode. Its primary function is to provide user and disc category information. Data Q mode 1 provides two kinds of information depending on its position. For a track, Data Q provides running time. In the lead-in track, Data Q has a table of contents which holds track numbers, time of the tracks, and the starting points of the tracks. The starting-point time is expressed in terms of absolute time, which is the actual running time on the disc. During the playback of the lead-in section the contents section is continuously repeated. Each of the individual tables is repeated three times. Data Q in the program and lead-out area holds track numbers, indices (which are subdivision numbers within a track), the time within a track, and the absolute disc time. The number of display features can differ, depending on the individual compact disc.

Regardless of the number of display features on your player, the Data Q information on the disc allows time to be displayed in two ways. Most players display individual track time by setting the track time to zero at the start of the track. Time increases until the pause between the tracks is reached and then decreased to zero at the end of the pause. In this case, track time also includes the lead in and lead out. Absolute time can be used to note the total time of the selection played, as well as the time remaining for the unplayed selections. Data Q mode 1 for absolute time is set to zero at the start of the first music track and increases to the end of the program lead out. Both Data Q mode 1 times are displayed as minutes, seconds, and frames. The system counts 75 frames per second. This type of display (minutes, seconds, frames) is found usually only on the higher-end CD players. The "frames" indication is not a direct representation of the data frames on the disc. After all, the data frame rate is 7350 hertz. The frame display is really just the smallest unit which the system control can resolve, and it is that time required to read one complete subcode block. This makes sense, since the Q channel can be updated only once in every subcode block, that is, once every 98 data frames. The following formula shows how the "frames" display is derived.

$$\frac{7350 \text{ data frames per second}}{98 \text{ data frames per subcode block}} = 75 \text{ subcode blocks per second}$$

Manufacturers like to use the term "frame" instead of "subcode block."

Data Q mode 2 reads out a catalog number in the form of a standard bar code. Data Q mode 3 is found only in the program area. It contains an International Standard Recording Code (ISRC), which gives the year of recording, serial number, country code, and owner code of the music.

SUMMING IT UP: REVIEWING THE FRAME

An audio disc data frame is the basic unit of information for the compact disc system. The frame contains audio information from both the left and right audio input channels. Each frame contains six samples per channel, for twelve samples total. Each sample is a digital representation of an analog audio signal. The transformation from analog to digital is done by a 44.1-kilohertz sampling signal. The result of the digital conversion is a 16-bit word, which is split into two 8-bit symbols. The 8-bit audio symbols are then converted to 14-bit symbols through the process of EFM. This process allows for the restriction of both the high-frequency and low-frequency content of the data stream. To help prevent playback errors, parity words, four per channel, allow for error concealment in the event of a dropout. As each symbol, regardless of containing audio or parity information, can be considered as an individual element, a method is required to make a consistent, undistorted transition between information elements. This is the responsibility of three merging bits positioned between each element. To complete the frame, both sync and control information are added to the frame. Sync is composed of 24 bits and serves the dual function of identifying the start of the frame and enabling the compact disc system to maintain a consistent rotation speed. The control symbol is composed of 14 bits in the same manner as the data or parity symbols because of EFM. The information contained within the control bits is related to duration and titling of the selections. Information contained in the control channels becomes meaningful only after 98 frames have been read.

ONE FRAME: COUNTING THE BITS

Let's get a look at just how many data bits there are within a frame. First there is the 24-bit sync word followed by its 3 merging bits. Then there is the first group of 12 audio symbols, each 14 bits long, and each with merging bits. Next are the four P parity words, each 14 bits long with merging bits. Following this, there is the second group of 12 audio symbols and merging bits. Last are the four Q parity words, each 14 bits long and with 3 merging bits so that it can be joined to the next frame. All of this results in 588 data bits per frame. Since there are 7350 frames that occur in one second, we can see that the data bit rate is 4.321 megabits per second.

Sync word	$24 + 3 =$	27
Control word	$14 + 3 =$	17
Audio symbols	$(14 + 3) \times 12 =$	204
P parity	$(14 + 3) \times 4 =$	68
Audio symbols	$(14 + 3) \times 12 =$	204
Q parity	$(14 + 3) \times 4 =$	68
		588

An overall block diagram which shows the A/D conversion, multiplexing, error correction, control channel, and sync is shown in Fig. 4-8.

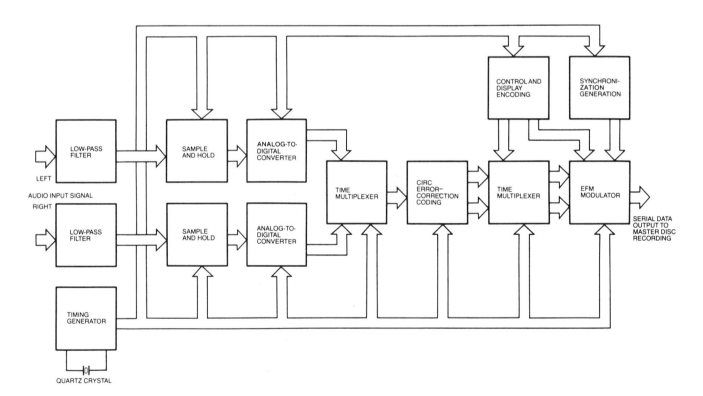

Fig. 4-8. CD encoding system. *(From Ken Pohlmann,* Principles of Digital Audio, *p. 223)*

5

The Construction of the Compact Disc

By offering approximately 60 minutes of playing time the compact disc contains roughly the same amount of audio information as the conventional long-playing record (although most LPs play less than 30 minutes per side). This one item represents the only similarity between the two systems. While the LP requires the use of both sides to hold information, the CD uses only one. While the diameter of the LP is nearly 300 millimeters, the CD diameter is only 120 millimeters. The dimensions of the CD are shown in Fig. 5-1.

The key to the high density of information packed into a small disc is the ability to compress information into a physical spot on the disc, known as a *pit*. The pit can be considered to be the equivalent of the audio groove on the LP. Pits represent all the audio, control, and sync information covered in chapter 4. Information is placed on the disc by creating a pit, and is recovered from the disc by optically reading the pit. Fig. 5-2 shows the dimensions and spacing of the pits. The quality of the signal read by the optical disc depends on the geometric structure of the pit. The signal output must be of sufficient high-frequency response in order to reproduce the audio and code information. In addition, it must also yield the servo tracking information.

Fig. 5-1. Physical characteristics of the compact disc. *(From Ken Pohlmann, Principles of Digital Audio, p. 221)*

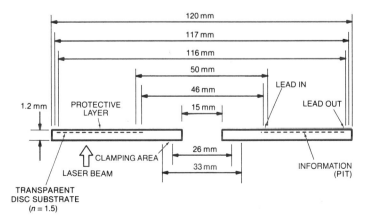

High-frequency recovery will result if the presence of a pit causes a reflective loss of the optical laser. This condition is dependent on the depth and width of the pit. In order for the reflected light to approach zero, the pit depth must equal a quarter of the laser wavelength. Pits positioned on the disc are separated by a physical spacing of 1.6 micrometers. This is also called *track pitch*. In order to properly recover the information represented by the pits, the system tracking must stay on the track of concern and not jump to an adjacent track, a mere 1.6 micrometers away.

The one variable in pit geometry is the pit length. It is a direct result of the EFM signal used in the encoding process. If we were to ignore all the encoded peripheral data such as parity, merging, and control bits, we would see that the pit length is a reflection of the information found in the original analog signal. This variation results in pit length values between 0.833 and 3.054 micrometers. The minimum variation from one pit length to the next cannot be less than 0.278 micrometer. The actual pit depth will be determined later during the development of the master disc. The final criterion will be judged by the resulting wavelength of the laser beam. The actual physical depth of the pit on the disc master will depend on the ability of the developing chemicals to wash away the surface coating. The

width of the pit, along with the angle of the pit slope, will depend not only on the developing process but also how the laser beam is focused on the master disc during the recording process. Track pitch is a product of the rotating speed of the master disc and the velocity at which the signal is applied to the disc. The standards for both of these fix the track pitch at 1.6 micrometers.

CREATING THE DISC

The recording process starts by receiving the output of the encoder, complete with the cross-interleave Reed-Solomon code and eight- to fourteen-bit modulation (EFM). Cutting the signal onto the disc medium is done in a manner similar to that of the drive coils that control the cutting stylus of the audio LP disc. The encoded high-frequency signal is used to control an acousto-optical modulator, which in turn modulates the laser light beam. Data is serially fed to the optical modulator. The beam is fed to an objective lens and onto the medium of the master disc. Because the disc is constantly rotating, a highly accurate focusing system, controlled by a servo system, is required to maintain accurate signal writing. The focusing

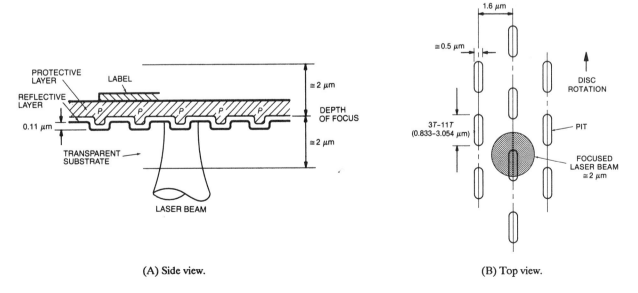

(A) Side view.   (B) Top view.

Fig. 5-2. The pits in a track. *(From Ken Pohlmann,* Principles of Digital Audio, *p. 221)*

system is actually two separate systems. The first is a separate diode laser, which guides the objective lens for the best possible beam focus. A second focusing system uses the reflected light from the disc. This light is used to monitor the beam and to make fine focusing adjustments. The exposed master disc is rotated while a developing solution is applied to the selected areas contacted by the laser. The developing solution is applied to the disc until the pit geometry reflecting the input signal is created. Additional lasers are used during the developing process. By focusing these lasers on the pits the pit development can be monitored by measuring the intensity of the reflected light.

facturing process. Any defects that result in the production of a father can be passed on to preceding generations with a greater amount of error. Distortions in pit geometry can cause a number of problems, such as high-frequency modulation amplitude variations. Tracking problems are associated with variations in track pitch, and playback signal noise with instabilities in track formations.

The pit surface of the disc is then coated with a layer of aluminum, which gives it its reflective characteristic. This surface is protected with a coating of lacquer. Finally, the label is applied and the center hole cut.

DEVELOPING THE DISC

The surface of the disc is covered by a light-sensitive chemical which aids in transferring the optical laser beam focused on its surface. After it is exposed to the laser beam the disc is rotated through a developing solution, which will erode the exposed surface units. In this way the pits are created. The pits are coated through a silvering process.

At this point the CD disc master, used to press playback discs, is formed. This disc carries the negative structure of the playback disc. The father disc is used to stamp a number of positive mothers. The mother in turn is used to produce a number of negative stampers, or sons. The son is then used to impress the surface of the playback disc we purchase.

The reason for using stampers instead of directly cutting the disc from the negative father is due to the limited amount of pressing that can be achieved prior to the father losing its precise physical characteristics. Since the father is expensive to produce, by using the limited number of pressings available from the father a greater number of mothers and stampers can be produced and used to create a larger number of final product discs than can be created from a single father. Fig. 5-3 shows the CD manu-

CHECKING THE DISC FOR ERRORS

The critical requirements of disc manufacturing necessitate subjecting the disc to quality control. Because the signals recorded on the disc are digital, checking the disc's quality can be achieved by comparing the impressed signal to an established group of codes. Although there is no standard industry agreed-on procedure for checking discs, the standard manner in which data is transferred to the disc sets up certain parameters. The conditions that should be checked for are the table of contents (TOC). The TOC contained in the Data Q mode 1 channel of the lead in of the disc must indicate the total number of tracks, location duration of each music track, and total disc playing time. Mode 2 offers the identification number for that specific disc, and mode 3 the ISR number assigned to that disc. Errors are measured in terms of the data remaining constant over the prescribed period of time.

As the TOC is repeated three times in the lead-in section of the track, there are two possible checks that can be performed. The first is that the TOC really does occur three times. The second is that the start time for each music track listed in the TOC corresponds to the actual start time of each track.

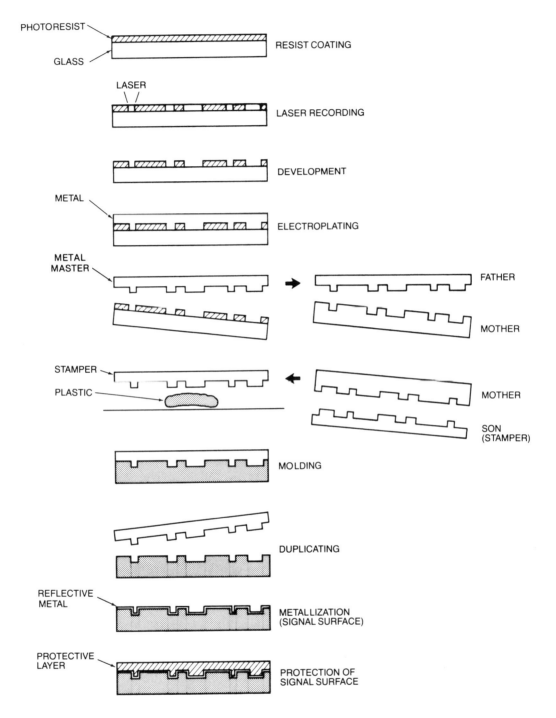

Fig. 5-3. CD manufacturing process. *(From Ken Pohlmann,* Principles of Digital Audio, *p. 235)*

THE P FLAG

The P flag subcode is set to a specific value, depending on its position in relationship to the musical track. In the pause interval between the musical selections the value is 1, and 0 for music tracks. During the lead out after the musical track the P flag alternates between 1 and 0 every 0.5 second, or at a rate of 2 hertz. The value of the P subcode is checked against these known fixed values.

The misreading of code errors can be caused by either dust or scratches. The error recovery is limited to those that can be corrected by parity bit checks and signal interleaving. When the number of errors per second exceeds the ability of these systems to correct, a block code error will result. These types of errors can cause frequency distortion or system mistracking. The latter causes the playback laser beam to misread the audio data. This results in a loss of high frequencies.

Each one of these errors can be displayed on a computer terminal or a computer-printed readout. The information listed can include the number of times and duration of each fault.

6

An Overview of the System

Regardless of the ability of the compact disc to produce high-quality audio signals in the digital mode, it is still dependent on the original recording medium. If the source were recorded in analog form, then much of the advantage of digital high-frequency response would be lost, no matter what the digital playback quality of the disc. While digital audio playback can produce high-quality audio it cannot correct defects present in the original source signal.

Although the compact disc medium is an excellent method for high-quality audio playback, it is better suited as a storage medium than a production medium. The laser disc is not erasable. Once the father is made it cannot be changed, and the creation of fathers is expensive. In addition, the production of a musical selection usually requires the recording of many individual audio tracks, after which the tracks are mixed to produce the final product. Compact discs are only capable of recording a maximum of four channels, far short of the 16- and 24-channel studio production recorders. The recording signals are then used to guide the optical lens system that creates the master disc.

Conventional audio production still requires the use of a tape medium. At this point a paradox is created. If a musical selection requires any conventional type of postproduction, then direct recording to disc cannot be used economically. The solution lies in the recording of digital audio signals on magnetic tape. The practicality of recording PCM signals on tape is more easily stated than put into actual use. Recording the high frequencies necessary in reproducing the rapid rate of transitions that compose the PCM signal requires a high signal writing speed. This term defines that rate at which signals are transferred from the head to the tape. Low-frequency recordings produce a low rate of signal transfer. As a result, a slow tape speed can be used and still accommodate the complete cycle. If the audio frequency increases without an associated increase in the tape speed, the positive cycle of the signal can be recorded on the same space as the negative cycle. When this occurs the resulting signal output is zero. The simple solution would be to increase the speed of the tape. This is possible up to the point that the amount of tape and size of the reels become impractical. The solution to recording high frequencies lies in increasing the writing speed by increasing both the tape and head speeds. In standard audio recording, the head used to transfer the audio signals is stationary. The audio signals are recorded on linear continuous tracks. Recording very high frequency signals required developing a system that used a method other than a stationary head structure.

THE DIGITAL AUDIO RECORDER

Fortunately such a system already existed. In the early 1970s Japanese manufacturers made a major breakthrough in the recording of video signals. This breakthrough was significant in that until this time the recording of video signals commonly required large-size recorders, using expensive 2-inch (5.08-centimeter) tape. The cost of the recorders came close to $100 000. This new technology reduced to ³/₄ inch (1.905 centimeters) the size of the tape, along with the size of the recorder. Even more importantly, the cost of video recording was reduced to approximately $2000. The process behind this recorder is known as *helical-scan recording*. It allowed the high-frequency video rates, which can reach 4 megahertz, to be recorded, by transferring the signal onto tape through two heads mounted on a rotating cylinder. The tape contacts the heads by being partially wrapped around the drum cylinder. As a result the increase in tape writing speed allows the recording of a high range of frequencies. Fig. 6-1 shows a VCR tape transport.

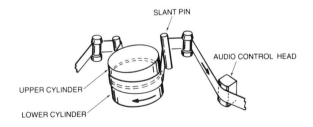

Fig. 6-1. Tape transport for helical scan in video cassette recorder. *(From Ken Pohlmann, Principles of Digital Audio, p. 148)*

The technology used in this method of recording was transferred over to audio. The result is R-DAT, rotary digital audio tape. Like its video counterpart, the audio rotary audio disc mastering system uses video vertical sync as a reference for the rotating head and custom tape speeds. The digital audio information is recorded at the horizontal and vertical video rates. Each rotating head records on tracks of audio. The number of recorded audio tracks during one rotation is determined by the number of heads used. This method has one drawback. A large burst can affect a number of recorded data samples. This increases the duration of simple interleaving over that found in the compact disc. Larger interleaving requires larger memory.

THE MASTERING SYSTEM

The digital audio recorder is only part of the disc mastering system. As its only function is record digital signals, it must be preceded by a processor that is responsible for converting analog audio to digital. The real advantage in recording digital audio signals on magnetic tape is the capability to edit. With an editing accuracy down to 363 microseconds, the equivalent of 16 words can be achieved. Editing accuracy is achieved through the same means used in video. A reference code developed by the Society of Motion Picture and Television Engineers (SMPTE) labels each of the audio fields with its own unique number. Known as time code, it is usually recorded by a stationary head on a longitudinal track. Editing is done by marking the in and out points in terms of the SMPTE time code. The audio master process would not be complete if a method were not available for recording the P and Q subcode information. This information is not included on the tape until the final mastering point. Like the time code information, it is recorded on a longitudinal channel.

READING BACK THE SIGNAL

Reading back the signals represented by the pits of the compact disc requires greater accuracy than can be achieved by a conventional mechanical pickup system. Instead the signal is read out by a beam of concentrated light, known as a laser beam. Light amplified by stimulated emission of radiation (laser) is capable of reading with a great deal of resolution. Readings are possible down to 1 micrometer.

The laser is guided on the disc by two different servo systems. The first controls the movement of the optical assembly as it travels from the inside of the disc to the outer edge. The second servo system controls the positioning of the lens focus in order to achieve the required detail reading of the disc pits. The main processing system consists of digital-to-analog conversion, which yields the sound we hear.

PLAYING BACK THE COMPACT DISC

The changes in reflected light produce a high-frequency sine wave. This waveform is shaped into a square wave. The transitions are sampled and compared with an internally generated reference signal. The reading of the pits is an indication of the speed of the disc. Control of disc speed is important; the servo must compensate in speed for the change in disc diameter as the laser moves from the inner to outer diameter. In order to maintain consistent reading of the signal pits, the servo system must slow the rotation speed from 500 to 200 revolutions per minute.

After the rotation speed is controlled, the signal-reading process starts by reading the synchronizing word which marks the start of the frame. At this point the control and display information is separated from the audio.

AUDIO PROCESSING

Next the signal is passed to an 8- to 14-bit (EFB) demodulator. This reverses the conversion process that occurred during recording. During 14- to 8-bit modulation the signal is also subject to error correction. The signal parity bits are used to either correct errors or, if correction is not possible, to conceal the errors.

Error Correction

Error correction is made easier because the CIRC code interleaved the signal during recording. The errors present in the original signal are then spread out over a number of nonadjacent frames. Error correction and detection during the playback process use two different decoders. The first decoder makes use of the parity symbols (P symbols). Correction is limited to the duration of symbol errors. Durations of one-symbol errors can be corrected without requiring the system to set up a pointer flag. At the two-symbol duration the correction system sets up a pointer with a value of 1. This alerts the rest of the correction system that the possibility of miscorrection exists. If problems are found in durations greater than two symbols, all the symbols in the frame will carry a pointer value of 1. The signal is then passed on to decoder number 2, which reads the 24 data symbols and uses four Q parity bits for correction. Decoder number 2 uses decoder number 1's correction flags to estimate the probability of miscorrection. Correction is performed when the probability of miscorrection is low. When it is high decoder number 2 will perform correction and output its own set of pointers. Finally, if decoder number 2 determines that the error is too long for it to correct, it will output an uncorrected signal with pointer. During final decoding an analysis will be made of decoder 2's pointers. CIRC correction can be used over a range of 14 frames, which are the equivalent of 450 symbols, and a duration of 1.9 milliseconds.

When errors occur which are greater than can be corrected by CIRC, a decision will be made to directly output or mute the signal, or use a process known as *interpolation*. This process occurs for uncorrectable signal durations of up to 48 frames. Interpolation uses the previous and following signal values to correct to a new value which is the average between the two. The result is to as closely as possible approximate the missing information to the original value. If this correction did not take place, the sudden change in signal amplitude would produce a pop or a click. If the distribution of errors does not spread out the bit errors into a manageable duration, the bit values are set to 0 and the output is muted.

CONTROL AND DISPLAY

The control and display information and Q information, which contains the table of contents, time index number, and control functions, are fed into a random-access memory (RAM). Accessing the information from the RAM is done by entering the request through the front control panel. After the request is read and processed the appropriate information is taken from the RAM and displayed through a series of front-panel light-emitting diodes.

DIGITAL-TO-ANALOG CONVERSION

The end product of signal correction still leaves the audio signal in digital form. Prior to our hearing the output signal from the compact disc the signal must be converted from digital to analog. This process consists of reading the digital word, converting into a voltage, and holding that signal until the next digital word is sampled and converted. The analog signal is reconstructed by connecting the individual voltage levels so that the complete audio signal is produced.

The transitions between the different digital points occur at high-frequency rates that extend beyond that of the 20-kilohertz audible limit. If these frequencies where allowed to pass into the analog audio input, it would cause distortion. These over-the-limit frequencies must be suppressed by at least 50 decibels for the 20-hertz to 20-kilohertz analog audio range. It is possible to eliminate these higher frequencies through the use of an analog filter. The tolerances of these filters, however, would have to be so tight that the increased costs of the filters would add to the final compact disc pricing. These analog filters are, however, found in many CD player models. Instead of using a final output stage analog fil-

ter, some players use a digital filter which is positioned prior to the digital-to-analog converter. This digital filter operates at a frequency four times higher than the 44.1-kilohertz analog-to-digital sampling frequency. Studies have shown that at four times the baseband frequency most of the high-frequency harmonics that cause distortion can be easily filtered out. This four times oversampling procedure moves the 44.1-kilohertz sampling noise up the frequency spectrum by a factor of 4–to become 176.4 kilohertz, as shown in Fig. 6-2. This practice allows a simple low-pass filter to be used for final filtering after the digital-to-analog converter.

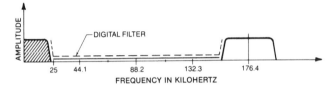

Fig. 6-2. Oversampling multiplies the sampling frequency. *(From Ken Pohlmann, Principles of Digital Audio, p. 116)*

A 176.4-kilohertz filtering rate is accomplished by clocking one of the 44.1-kilohertz sampling periods four times. For a typical clocking of a sample period a value of 1 is assigned to the first clock followed by 000. This method gave rise to the term used to describe this method as "oversampling." A block diagram is shown in Fig. 6-3. The actual operation of the oversampling filter performs four add and delay operations within one of the 44.1-kilohertz sample periods. The time that it takes for 176.4 cycles to occur has another effect on the system. During the oversampling, clocking delays are used so that the one sampling period of the 176.4 kilohertz occurs at the same time the fourteenth bit is passing through the oversampling filter. As a result the 16-bit, 44.1-kilohertz sampling signal is input to the digital oversampling filter at the same time the 14-bit, 176.4-kilohertz sample pulse occurs at the filter output. However, due to oversampling, the 14-bit output is just as accurate as the original 16-bit word, because the average value of the multiplied 14-bit samples equals that of untreated 16-bit samples. The advantages of the system over that of direct 16-bit analog filtering are not limited to just costs. First, digital filtering does not have the phase distortion characteristics associated with analog filters. Second, the rate of filtering is directly taken from the oversampling clocking rate, so that any problem that is a result of servo distortion will not be a factor.

Another inherent result of oversampling is the reduction of the quantization noise that occurs during the digital-to-analog conversion. Because the signal is sampled at a rate of four times the original, each sample will therefore contain one-fourth the original noise energy. This equates to an improvement of the signal-to-noise ratio by 6 decibels. This system accounts for the extremely high signal-to-noise ratios found in compact disc systems. CD signal-to-noise ratios greater than 95 decibels are common.

In digital-to-analog conversion the analog signal components are reconstructed through resistive ladder networks fed by transistors. The incoming digital values generate currents which are switched by bit switchers. For this type of system there are a number of limitations. Each one of the digital currents must work itself into a precise resistive load. This weighed load must be switched with a great deal of accuracy. Any variations in the output load or switcher timing will produce a distorted output. Most important is that this type of digital-to-analog conversion requires extremely precise values of resistors, which, on a mass-production basis, are difficult to manufacture reliably.

DYNAMIC-ELEMENT MATCHING

As the number of bits required to convert a digital signal to analog increases, the weighing of the elements that control the current must take on a greater degree of accuracy. The current-weighing elements must be precisely timed in order to produce the correct output signal. This becomes extremely difficult and costly as we approach the 14- to 16-bit ranges.

As digital-to-analog conversion in the compact disc uses 16 bits it must rely on a higher-resolution conversion system. This approach is known as *dynamic-element matching*. The system uses a divide-by-2 stage. The timing of the division is controlled by a clock generator, as shown in Fig. 6-4. The output currents, of which we'll refer to as I_1 and I_2, have the same mean value, differing only in phase. The output of the circuit is an exact 1:2 current ratio, and therefore the circuit is a 2-bit current divider. Within this divider further current division is performed by a grouping of current-weighed transistors. In order to minimize signal loss that can occur during this process, the output of each of the divider stages is fed to a network of Darlington switches. The arrangement of these Darlington switches also allows the currents to be mixed by activating the switches with a shift register, which is shown in Fig. 6-5.

Next, each of the weighed-current networks is cascaded. The current referenced serves as the most significant bit current and each of the bit current networks provides 2 bits. This process is used to create the analog voltage signal output for bits 1 through 10. The four least significant bits, numbers 11 to 14, are then created by means of passive current division, as shown in Fig. 6-6. Looking at the analog output signal, we can see that it still contains a pulse characteristic which is the result of being created from a digital form. In order for the signal to have a cleaner form, a sample and hold circuit converts the pulses to a square-wave signal, as shown in Fig. 6-7. Finally,

Fig. 6-3. Digital filter with oversampling. *(From Ken Pohlmann, Principles of Digital Audio, p. 115)*

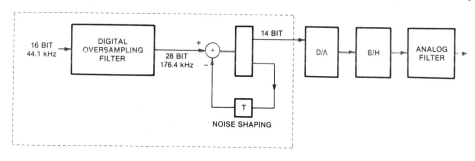

a low-pass filter smooths out the rough edges of individual stairs to create a smooth sine wave (Fig. 6-8).

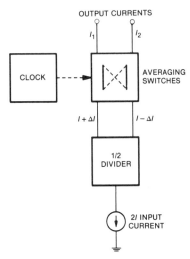

Fig. 6-4. Dynamic-element matching current divider stage. *(From Ken Pohlmann,* Principles of Digital Audio, *p. 107)*

SERVO SYSTEMS

As noted for the digital-to-analog process, the compact disc system has the limited ability to compensate for distortion of approximately 1.9 milliseconds. These distortions are expected to occur due to disc reading problems. Far more serious problems can occur if an accurate and consistent reading of the bit information from the disc cannot be maintained. This is the function of the compact disc's servo system. In reality the servo system is made up of four different systems. The *focus servo* is used to guide the laser beam so that it can read the pits accurately. Even though the placement of pits is precisely determined by the stamping process, distortion can occur due to warping of an individual disc. The tracking servo positions the focus beam on the individual track spirals that contain the pits. During disc rotation, minor variations in speed can result in major changes in the rate at which the pit information is read. The focus servo operates by reading the shape of the returning (or reflected) beam. The shape of the returning laser beam will create a positive or negative servo voltage. When the returning beam takes the shape of a circle the correction voltage is zero. When the laser reading produces an elliptical shape, a minus or plus correction voltage is created. The system operates by a grouping of photodiodes which reads these shapes and produces the correction voltage. From the photodiode array the diodes' signals are combined to produce the voltage differential.

The *tracking servo* system operates to keep the optics on track at all times. As the disc makes one revolution the track advances toward the outer periphery of the disc by the distance of one track pitch, or 1.6 micrometers. The tracking servo actually consists of a drive circuit which, when sending current through a coil attached to the lens, shifts the position of the lens. Tracking error is different for the two major types of laser optics found in CD players: the three-beam system and the single-beam system. This problem is more closely examined in chapter 7.

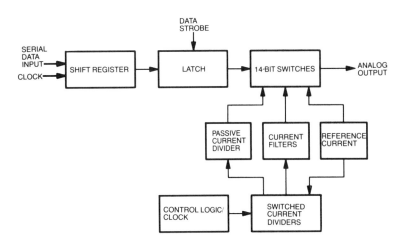

Fig. 6-5. Dynamic-element matching D/A converter block diagram. *(From Ken Pohlmann,* Principles of Digital Audio, *p. 108)*

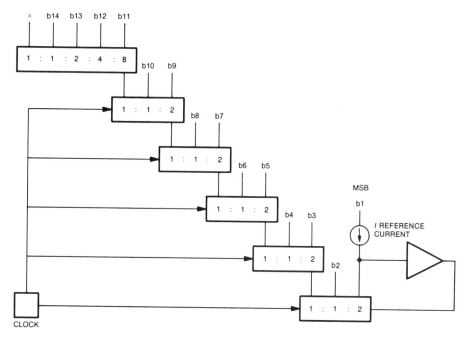

Fig. 6-6. Dynamic-element matching current divider cascade. *(From Ken Pohlmann,* Principles of Digital Audio, *p. 108)*

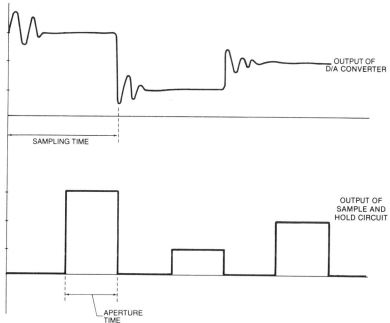

Fig. 6-7. A sample and hold circuit is used to avoid glitches present at the output of a D/A converter. *(From Ken Pohlmann,* Principles of Digital Audio, *p. 110)*

The *spindle motor servo* is that circuitry responsible for actually spinning the disc. Unlike motor drive servo systems found in other types of audio and video systems, the spindle servo drive system of a compact disc system has additional functions. Data from the compact disc must be read out at a constant rate. As the disc rotates, however, the circumference of the tracks continually changes from the inner to outer diameter of the disc. This requires that the spindle motor drive speed change as the laser tracks the disc, from 500 revolutions per minute at the inner diameter to 200 revolutions per minute at the outer diameter. The goal of the system is to read the pits at a constant speed. Control for the spindle motor servo is taken from the synchronizing pulse recorded at the beginning of each frame. When the spindle motor

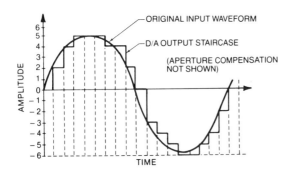

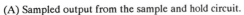

(A) Sampled output from the sample and hold circuit.

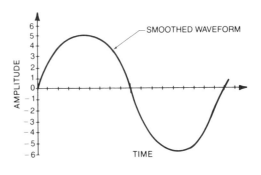

(B) Waveform from output low-pass filter.

Fig. 6-8. Smoothing the output from the sample and hold circuit. *(From Ken Pohlmann,* Principles of Digital Audio, *p. 113)*

servo is rotating at the proper speed this synchronizing pulse produces a frequency of 7.35 kilohertz. This sync pulse is read by the laser and compared with an internal reference. Variations between the two create an error signal.

Finally, modifications to the various servos are used for modes other than play. These special modes include, search, skip, pause, and so on. The response of the servo circuits is altered so that servo overcompensation does not occur. Certainly, large tracking error signals produced by the tracking servo circuit must be ignored when search is engaged. Otherwise the servo would actually fight the search process.

7

The Laser Pickup

The most critical area of any playback system is that of the pickup, or reading device. We are all familiar with the magnetic cartridge and stylus used in the playback of conventional LPs. The magnetic head is the reading device used in audio and video tape recording systems. We have grown accustomed to the fact that these devices wear with use, that is, they are consumable. The same characteristic is true for the CD system. The playback reading device used in CD is a wear-prone consumable item which is manufactured to quite high precision but has a much higher level of sophistication than that of the LP stylus. The playback element for CD is a laser system with its associated optics.

First, let us be clear on why laser light was chosen to be the pickup medium. Laser light is light energy consisting of waves which are all of the same frequency and are all in phase. This light is called *coherent* light. In contrast, the light from an LED, incandescent bulb, or fluorescent lamp is noncoherent, that is, light energy from a range of frequencies is emitted, with random phases. This is shown in Fig. 7-1. It is the single-frequency, in-phase property that is desired when reading the pits of the compact disc. Ham radio and CB operators may identify this kind of

property because of their first-hand experience in tuning antennas. To tune an antenna to a particular frequency, i.e., wavelength, the antenna's length must be cut or adjusted to become a multiple of that particular frequency. When this is achieved, the peaks and valleys of the rf energy can be detected by running a fluorescent bulb along the antenna, as the bulb will illuminate at the peaks. In this case the antenna is tuned and is carrying rf energy of just one frequency, or one wavelength, and in phase.

The beam from the laser diode is tuned by the physical dimensions of the diode's construction, and typically the wavelength is in the area of 800 nanometers. The total light output from the diode is critical in the sense that if the emitted beam varies in intensity, it could adversely affect the playback signal. Therefore the output from the laser diode is regulated in order to provide a constant light output. Remember that it is the coherence of the light that is important, and that a tuned system (like a radio antenna) can have peaks and valleys along its path. Technicians and engineers know this condition more commonly as a standing wave.

With these ideas in mind, let's look at the laser path of a typical CD player. Once ener-

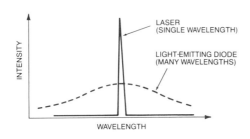

(A) Laser light contains only one wavelength.

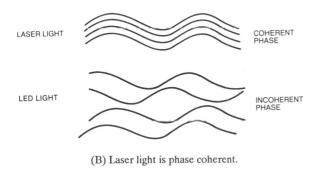

(B) Laser light is phase coherent.

Fig. 7-1. Properties of laser light. *(From Ken Pohlmann,* Principles of Digital Audio, *p. 239)*

gized, the diode laser will emit laser light energy of about 800 nanometers in wavelength, which places the light in the infrared band. It is of the utmost importance to realize that the laser beam is indeed invisible to the human eye but is still capable of causing injury and damage. *Never look directly into the path of the laser light* to determine if the laser is working. Even if the unit is working properly, and there is no need to observe the laser, still take precautions to prevent exposure of your eyes to the beam. Safety is always the first rule of any troubleshooting endeavor.

Once the beam is emitted from the diode housing, it will go through several optical stages. The first of these optical elements is the collimator lens, which really is a glass element used to help to converge the diode's light which normally tends to diverge. Just because the light is coherent, this doesn't mean that it won't diverge as it leaves its source, as noncoherent light does. The collimator directs the beam into a parallel, nondiverging beam. The next step is one which will determine the type of optical system used, which we more commonly know as the three-beam or single-beam system. From this

point on, the two systems will be treated individually.

THREE-BEAM SYSTEMS

After the beam is refined by the collimator, it is then passed through a diffraction grating lens which serves to split the beam up into three separate beams, as shown in Fig. 7-2. Quite interestingly, one can see firsthand what effect the diffraction grating lens has, by removing one from a defective laser/optical assembly, and carefully looking through it. When the grating is placed close to the eye, the viewer will see three distinct replicas of whatever object is being viewed, somewhat like the multi-image filters used in modern photography. The most intense image seen by the eye is called the main, or center, image. The two other, less intense, images are on either side of the main image. This exact effect is placed on the beam that enters the grating lens. Three beams will exit, with the center or main beam being the strongest, and the two side beams having less intensity (see Fig. 7-2). It can be stated now that the main beam is used for the reading of the track of pits currently being played, and is also used for playing back the data. The two side beams are used to read the same track, but they are situated just ahead of and behind the main beam. All three of these beams are sent up to the disc, and are reflected back to playback photodiodes.

The three beams, coming from the grating lens, are next passed through a beam-splitting prism (BSP), as shown in Fig. 7-3. The purpose of this element is to separate the emitted beams from the reflected beams. Constructed of two individual but joined elements, the beam-splitting prism is, in basic terms, an optical separator, or gate, which passes or reflects laser light, depending on the polarization of the laser light. Most people are familiar with polarizing sunglasses, those which use polarized optical lenses to pass just certain kinds of light. These sunglass lenses contain many thousands of stripes, too small and closely spaced for the human eye to see. But they

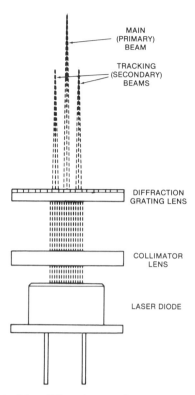

Fig. 7-2. The diffraction grating lens splits the laser light into multiple beams. *(From Ken Pohlmann, Principles of Digital Audio, p. 240)*

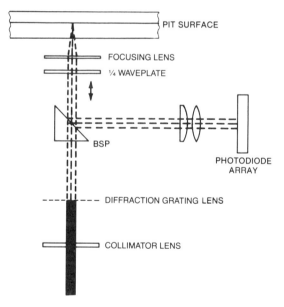

Fig. 7-3. Three-beam tracking optical path. *(From Ken Pohlmann, Principles of Digital Audio, p. 246)*

of the light wave occur. (Consider wiggling a clothesline; is it wiggling in the vertical or horizontal direction?) Direct light and glaring reflections tend to have different planes of polarization. Thus polarized sunglasses work by blocking the glaring reflected light, whose plane of polarization won't allow it to pass through the stripes of the lens.

This same principle holds true for the beam-splitting prism. The plane of polarization from the emitted light allows it to pass directly through the prism and onto a one-quarter waveplate. (One-quarter refers to the distance of one-fourth of the wavelength.) This element actually changes the plane of polarization of the emitted beams. The polarization changes from that of being planar (flat, within one plane) to being circular. The importance of this element is that it will also affect the reflected beams, and the total change in the plane of polarization will allow the prism to separate the reflected beams from the emitted beams. Once the plane of polarization has been made circular by the one-quarter waveplate, it passes through the last element of the emission path, the focusing lens. The focusing lens is the one most readily identified by casual users, as it is the one which is exposed. This is the lens which is driven by the focus servo system. It is necessary to have a driven focusing lens because of the tolerance in the flatness of the disc. If the disc were absolutely flat, to the nanometer, there would be no need to drive the focusing lens. But since the disc cannot be made this flat, and since the disc must spin, it is the job of the optical assembly to compensate for an out-of-focus condition.

The Beams on the Disc

When the beams exit the focus lens, they will pass through the air, then onto the disc. The disc is, in reality, the final optical element in the path of the emitted beams. Most of the 1.2-millimeter thickness of the disc is needed and used as the final focusing lens in the system. The disc's polycarbonate has a refractive index of about 1.4. This means that the beam's size is reduced by a

are there, and tend to pass light of a particular plane of polarization. The plane of polarization could more conveniently be considered to be the direction or angle at which the peaks and valleys

factor of about 1000 when it reaches the pit surface. Considering the small size of the pits, it might be guessed that final focusing is all that is necessary to read the disc's information. But this 1000-to-1 reduction also accomplishes another desirable characteristic. Any fingerprints or scratches on the disc surface will have, in essence, 1000 times less of an influence at the pit surface. The effect is very similar to that experienced when one is wearing a pair of glasses (or sunglasses) which are mildly scratched. Because the eye is focused at a point well beyond the lens, the scratch is, for all intents and purposes, not noticed. (Small scratches on a camera lens, too, have little effect when the lens is focused at a relatively long distance.) By no means is this fact to be considered an excuse to expose the compact disc to more haphazard treatment than that which would be given to a conventional LP. Certainly, the long life of a CD can only be ensured if good care is provided. Continued storage in the "jewel box" type case is the best way to protect the disc.

The size of the main beam at the surface of the disc is approximately 1 mm. When the main beam is focused by a factor of 1000, its diameter is reduced to about 1 micrometer at the pit surface. The size of the beam here is larger than the 0.5 micrometer width of the pits (see Fig. 7-4). The two tracking beams are similarly affected by all the properties of the 1.4 refractive index of the polycarbonate. Because of the characteristic of the grating lens, the three beams, as they strike the surface of the pits, lie in a straight line, but slightly tilted. Fig. 7-5 shows the ideal case as the beams read the disc,

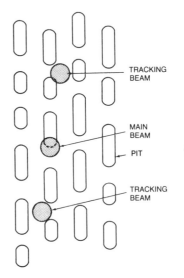

Fig. 7-5. Three-beam tracking beam alignment. *(From Ken Pohlmann,* Principles of Digital Audio, *p. 246)*

specifically, the main beam is centered on the track of concern, and the two tracking beams reading only a portion of the same track.

Tracking is accomplished by looking at the reflected tracking beams. Although we have not yet covered the reflection of the beams back into the optical assembly, we can see that if mistracking does occur, one of the tracking beams will start to become centered over its adjacent track. If the right tracking beam starts to pick up more pit area of the track, this can be detected, and suitably compensated. Likewise, if the optical assembly starts to mistrack in the opposite direction, the left tracking beam will cover more pit area from the track, and this too can be compensated.

Data recovery is accomplished by the amount of reflection of the main beam. The amount of reflection of the main beam is what can be called the intensity of the returning beam. The intensity of the returning beam is deter-

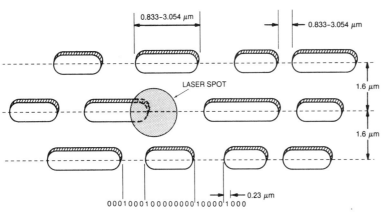

Fig. 7-4. Pits and laser beam on the disc. *(From Ken Pohlmann,* Principles of Digital Audio, *p. 228)*

mined by the pits, and their depth. In actuality, what was a pit, as cut on the master disc, appears as a flat in the final product, because the disc is read from the bottom side, as shown in Fig. 7-6. This is of no consequence, since it is the transition between pits and flats which represents the readout data, and not the pit itself or the flat itself. The depth of a pit is about 0.11 micrometer, or one-quarter of the wavelength of the laser light. The extra distance traveled by the beam when entering and reflecting back from a pit floor is equal to one-half of the wavelength of the laser light. This creates the 180° phase difference necessary to cause the laser beam to cancel itself, and ideally there would be no returning beam. Of course, tolerances in the manufacturing of the disc, player, lens assembly, etc., prohibit an ideal response, but there is a definite reduction in returning beam intensity as the main beam reads a pit.

Conversely, when the beam reads a flat, it is reflected, not canceled, and will be sensed by the playback photodetectors. It is this "turning on and off" of the returning beam which makes up the playback data. Continuing with the path of the beams, we find that they bounce off of the flats, and reenter the focusing lens. The path is next through the one-quarter waveplate, which will again change the plane of polarization of the beams. On the second trip of the light through

the one-quarter waveplate, the plane of polarization changes a total of 90°, and this allows the beam-splitting prism to direct the returning beam *not* down the same path as the sending beams, but off to the side, at a 90° angle to the sending beam. The returning beam will then pass through a cylindrical lens before reaching the photodiode array. The cylindrical lens will change the shape of the returning beams according to the condition of focus at the disc surface. The property of the cylindrical lens to change the shape of the returning beam is what allows for focus control.

The pattern of the three returning beams on the photodiode array is the same pattern that the sending beams make on the pit (or flat) surface. Fig. 7-7 shows the photodiode array with six segments, four grouped in the center for the main beam, and two others offset for the tracking beams. In an ideal in-focus condition, the pattern is that of circularly shaped beams on the segments. In the case of the four data segments, the beam spot illuminates a portion of all four segments equally. At the same time, the tracking segments are each partially illuminated. It is going to be these six segments where all data recovery is made, where tracking error is determined, and where focus error is determined.

If the set of three beams starts to mistrack, one of the tracking segments will have an

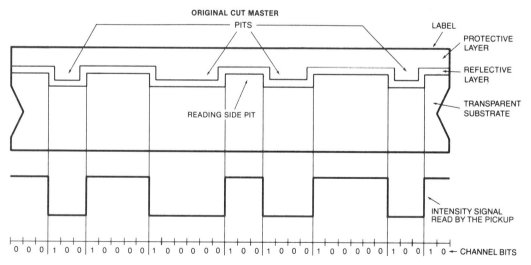

Fig. 7-6. What was a "pit" as originally cut on the master disc will be a "flat" as seen by the playback laser.
(From Ken Pohlmann, Principles of Digital Audio, *p. 222)*

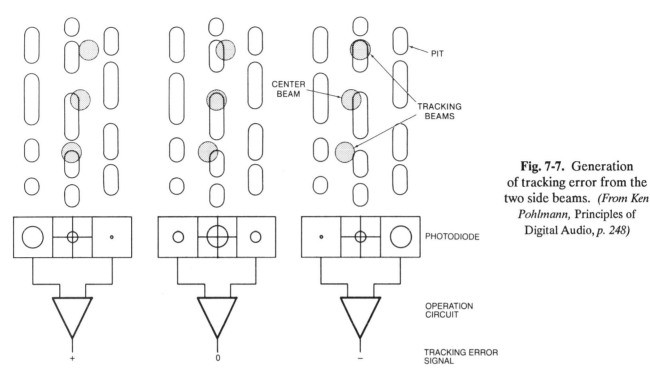

CENTER
BEAM

PIT

TRACKING
BEAMS

PHOTODIODE

OPERATION
CIRCUIT

TRACKING ERROR
SIGNAL

+ 0 −

Fig. 7-7. Generation of tracking error from the two side beams. *(From Ken Pohlmann,* Principles of Digital Audio, *p. 248)*

increased output, while the other one will diminish. Mistracking in the other direction will similarly reverse which tracking segment produces an increased output, and which segment output will diminish. Since the tracking beams are reading adjacent tracks, and will see pits and flats, data-type signals will be produced by the tracking segments. The outputs from these two segments are applied to a comparator. If both tracking segments are illuminated equally (on track), the comparator will deliver a zero output. If the tracking segments are unequally illuminated (off track), the output of the comparator will swing either positive or negative, depending on which segment receives more light.

The outputs from the tracking segments are, in most cases, connected to an integrated circuit in which the comparator and several amplification stages exist. The output from the integrated circuit is the actual tracking error signal. This is applied to the drivers and then to the tracking servo circuit.

The state of focus is determined by the shape of the returning main beam, as was mentioned. The four data segments are illuminated by a beam spot that varies in shape. In fact, some of the individual segments in the group may

receive very little illumination if a large deviation in focus occurs. More specifically, the shape of the returning main beam changes from that of being circular to that of being elliptical when an out-of-focus condition arises. An ellipse tilting toward the right results when the beam has focused too far (beyond the pit surface), and a left tilting ellipse results if the beam is focused too near. Elliptical patterns illuminate opposite pairs of the four data segments. The two sets of opposite pair segments are tied together, and these two outputs are applied to a comparator. And, like the comparator stage just described for tracking, the output would be zero for in-focus conditions, and would swing positive or negative for out-of-focus conditions. The amplified output would be used by the focus servo circuit.

For data recovery, the outputs of all four data segments are summed and become the playback data signal.

SINGLE-BEAM SYSTEMS

Fortunately, many of the processes described for the three-beam systems are also employed by single-beam systems. There is no diffraction grating lens after the diode laser and collimating lens, as there is no need to make three beams. This reduction in parts allows for a reduction in size of the optical assembly. At the pit surface of the disc the beam pattern is, of course, composed of just one spot. Returning from the disc, the beam will be reflected through the cylindrical lens, and onto the photodiode array. It is the photodiode array which is different in the case of the single beam.

New single-beam systems use a photodiode array composed of six segments, arranged differently, as shown in Fig. 7-8. The two segments labeled B1 and B2 are not used for tracking; they serve to add to the data recovery. The four segments in the center are used for focus and tracking. Focus is handled in the same way as was done for three-beam systems. Tracking, however, is determined differently. There are different methods employed by different manufacturers for this purpose, but that which will be described here is that found in the models from Technics. There is not an ideal cancellation of the beam when a pit is read, as was mentioned, and part of the reason is the size of the beam spot. The spot is about 1 micrometer, and is used to read pits that are about 0.5 micrometer wide. The beam pattern on the photodiodes, then, would have a "shadow" move through it as the pit passed by (not unlike the shadows made by moving clouds on a sunny day). Again, opposite pairs of the four center segments are tied together, and these two outputs are applied to a phase comparator (see Fig. 7-9). If the beam spot moves toward the left on the array, the lower left segment senses the moving shadow before the upper left segment does. This can be considered to be a "phase-lead" condition and produces, in this example, a

positive output from the phase comparator. If the beam pattern moves to the right, the shadow will pass the bottom right segment before the top right segment, and this will produce a "phase-lag" condition. In this example, the phase lag will produce a negative output from the comparator. The output from the comparator is used by the tracking servo circuits.

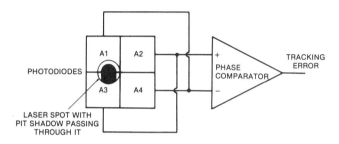

Fig. 7-9. Tracking error detection in a single-beam system.

WHY TWO SYSTEMS?

The wheel of progress can never be stopped or even slowed, so there can be no saying for sure that there won't be two-beam or four-beam systems. When CD players were first introduced several years ago, most of the systems were of the three-beam type. With the strive toward simplification and size reduction, more and more single-beam units have appeared. By omitting the grating lens the single-beam systems can be smaller and less expensive. Indeed, portable CD players attest to the fact of the reduced size in optics. Performance-wise, very little difference can be mentioned. Design engineers may boast about the inherent excellent trackability of three beams, but they will also have to acknowledge the larger photodiode array size and increased data output level of the single-beam systems. There is no "better" system, and as is the case for most types of consumer products, there never will be a "best."

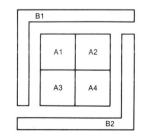

Fig. 7-8. Photodiode array used by Technics single-beam players.

POTENTIAL PLAYBACK PROBLEMS

Regardless of which beam system is used, the process of playback is critical. It is still amazing to realize the size of the pits and the tracks that are supposed to be read without flaw. All of the careful interleaving and parity word generation is used to fully compensate for what might happen during optical playback.

Even despite the refractive properties of the polycarbonate plastic, fingerprints, smudges, and scratches are likely to occur if the disc is handled in a less-than-ideal manner. The mass duplication process itself can certainly introduce microscopic defects. The error-correction scheme (CIRC) encoded into the master disc might be considered to be an excuse for more sloppy manufacturing methods, but this is certainly not true. Maintaining precision throughout the mass duplication process is difficult, but it is very meticulously achieved. Given this, there is still a chance for manufacturing defects. In other words, if it weren't for the CIRC scheme, we could expect to pay much, much more per compact disc, to obtain the same quality as with CIRC.

A perfectly functioning CD player would read any manufacturing defects that do occur, so that the error-correction scheme in players is necessary for this possibility alone. But like any other electromechanical system, new errors will be introduced at the time of playback. As has been stated, the single most common cause for playback errors is the effect caused by fingerprints, scratches, and the like. If severe enough, these can momentarily block the beam as it is going toward the pit surface. This would cause a dropout of information and can result in a form of noise such as a pop or click, or worse, permanent mistracking. (A "broken" CD *is* possible.)

It is also desirable to have the returning beam "modulated" by the presence of a pit as much as possible. We know that 100-percent cancellation of the beam is not practical, due mainly to beam size. If the pit depth is not approximately one-fourth the wavelength of the laser light, then the cancellation effect would be further diminished. Keep in mind that the primary purpose of the EFM operation is to keep the pit/flat transitions between $3T$ and $11T$, where T is the period of a clock cycle, so that a pit or flat can be no smaller than 3 clock cycles, and no longer than 11 clock cycles in length. (This clock is the master clock at 4.321 megahertz.) In effect, the EFM process guarantees that the optics will not have a very high frequency (high pit/flat transition rate), and also that the frequency will not get so low that tracking might be affected. (When a pit or flat is too long, the tracking beams will not read the adjacent track.) The EFM process allows for the use of simpler optics, thus keeping cost low.

Even with the advantages of EFM, the CIRC error-correction scheme is necessary to compensate for reading errors in playback. Dropouts can be corrected, but the inability to focus or the inability to track will produce errors too large for correction. Dirt on the focusing lens could certainly cause this. A warped disc or a bent spindle (onto which the disc is placed) could also be the cause. Large fingerprints or smudges should also be carefully removed if they are present. And there is such a thing as a defective compact disc. Yes, although it isn't not common, it is possible for just one disc to cause a problem on a player known to be in good condition. Beyond all these mechanical causes of problems, most of which may be avoided by good care and maintenance, may be the need to have the player serviced.

8

Circuit Descriptions, Part 1

In this chapter the circuits involving data pickup and recovery, along with the focus servo and the tracking servo, will be covered. In any description of this type the study must be confined to one particular model, as this is the only way that the different stages of the circuit will fit together and make sense. For this analysis we will examine the Technics SL-P2. This is a three-beam unit with full programmability, front-panel numeric display, direct access, and wireless remote control. In concept, many of these descriptions can carry over to other manufacturer's models, but in specific detail the SL-P2 system is totally unique. Technics, as well as most other manufacturers, use custom ICs of their own design and manufacture, so that their specific pinouts will not necessarily match that of other manufacturers' ICs.

THE LASER DIODE

The laser LED is part of a circuit called the automatic power control (APC), which is shown in Fig. 8-1. The LED isn't merely turned on when play is initiated; its output is constantly moni-tored for intensity and any variations are compensated. This is necessary so that any variations in beam intensity from its starting point will not be sensed as viable data (caused by the pits) at the photodiode array.

The command to turn on the laser LED, LD151, comes from the system control micro-processor, IC401. The command is called $\overline{\text{LD ON}}$ and is active low. When this low occurs, Q104 will be turned on, since bias can exist from the −5-volt supply through R105 and R106. Current through R103 and R104 will similarly turn on Q103. This action raises the emitter voltage of Q102, allowing it to operate along with Q101. The current path for the laser is from ground, through the laser, through Q101, to the −5-volt supply. Q101 is the pass regulator for the laser power. It is controlled by the conduction of Q102, and this is controlled by the response of the pin diode, which is sensing the laser light. If the laser power (intensity) increases, the resistance of the photoreceptive pin diode decreases. This tends to raise the base voltage of Q102, which reduces the base voltage of Q101, the pass regulator. As the base voltage of Q101 decreases, its current is cut back, thereby reducing the current through the laser LED. Variable resistor VR151 sets the bias

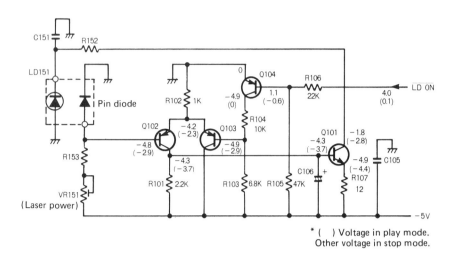

Fig. 8-1. Simplified schematic of laser automatic power control. *(Courtesy Technics)*

* ( ) Voltage in play mode.
Other voltage in stop mode.

level for Q102, and the action of the pin diode adds to, or subtracts from, this. Thus, VR151 sets the laser power. The power output of the laser is an adjustment that is made at the factory, and field or shop adjustment is not recommended. The adjustment is made so that there is ample, but not too high, beam power, in order to maximize laser LED life.

DISC SIGNAL (RF DATA) PICKUP

It is understood that without proper focus and tracking, there would be no data recovery, but since just one aspect of the playback recovery process can be analyzed at a time, we will start with that of data recovery, which involves the successive reading of the EFM signal and the table of contents. Remember that it is the EFM signal which contains the audio and parity information. The subcode channels contain the TOC, the Q channel running data, and the other data (unassigned at this time).

Successful beam operation will produce a playback RF signal from the photodiode array. The RF signal is a combination of sine waves varying in frequency from about 196 to 720 kilohertz. Of course, the ideal situation would be that an exact replica of the EFM signal appear at the output of the photodiodes. But in the "real world" we must accept the fact that there are tolerances in the following areas:

1. Disc flatness–Mass-produced discs are not always perfectly flat. This can aggravate focus problems.

2. Dust, dirt–Imperfections on the disc surface can alter the shape of the spot of laser light on the pit surface.

3. Aperture–The beam size on the pit surface is wider than the pits themselves. Therefore a nonideal response is generated.

4. Servo response time–Focus is achieved through an electronic circuit. There is no such thing as a servo circuit that is absolutely perfect–there is always some measurable response time, or "slop."

5. Pit shape–The pits are not steep in their depth, they are rounded, and this, perhaps more than anything else, prevents a squarewave EFM signal from appearing at the photodiodes.

These factors combine and result in a sinusoidal waveform being output by the photodiodes. This is more commonly called an RF (radio-frequency) signal. Nine discrete sine-wave frequencies are present in the RF signal. This is derived from the fact that a single pit/flat sequence can exist only between $3T$ (3 clock cycles) and $11T$ (11 clock cycles), thus there are only nine possible length values for a pit or flat. The highest sine-wave frequency is

$$4.321 \text{ MHz}/(3 \times 2) = 720 \text{ kHz}$$

and the lowest sine-wave frequency is

$$4.321 \text{ MHz}/(11 \times 2) = 196 \text{ kHz}$$

where

4.321 MHz = the data rate, the system clock,
$3T$ = the minimum pit/flat length,
$11T$ = the maximum pit/flat length.

Both clock cycle terms are multiplied by 2 since two successive $3T$ or $11T$ periods are needed to form a full sine wave.

The RF signal from the photodiodes is derived by combining the two opposite pairs of data segments. The opposite pairs are physically wired together, as shown in Fig. 8-2, and then enter IC103 at pins 13 and 14. They are summed and amplified internally and appear at pin 8, which provides officially the system RF signal. Next, the signal exits the optical board via connector BRT102, pin 9, and is applied to the main board through connector CN412, pin 9. This signal is visible at TJ402, one of the test points (see Fig. 8-3). The sinusoidal waveform is squared up by the combined action of four segments of IC301. The squared signal is visible at IC301, pin 8. This signal, and the following inverted signal at IC301, pin 4, are applied to an

integrator stage, made up by IC302 (section A) and associated components. Basically, this forms a negative-feedback network which, through integration, is sensitive mainly to changes in the dc level of the RF signal.

A simplified diagram is shown in Fig. 8-4. If the average dc level of the playback RF signal increases or decreases, the output of IC302, pin 7, will compensate. This action ensures that the RF signal will not drift out of the operating range of the rest of the decoder circuits, which could be caused by varying laser output or in the manufacturing of the disc.

The system clock signal is applied to IC306, pin 12. It is counted down to 2.16 megahertz (half the system clock value) and is similarly applied back up to the squaring stage, through R302, R304, to IC301, pin 12. This is done to prevent sudden unlock of the phase-locked loop circuit should a sizeable dropout occur. If a sudden loss of RF signal should occur, this clock will still be running, and tends to fill in for the missing data–but does not carry information. This means that an error will still be detected. It is not of sufficient level to interfere with the normal playback RF signal. Next, the signal is applied to IC303 (segment A), is inverted, and appears at

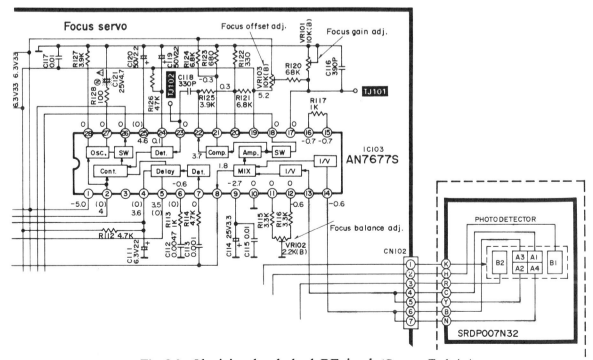

Fig. 8-2. Obtaining the playback RF signal. *(Courtesy Technics)*

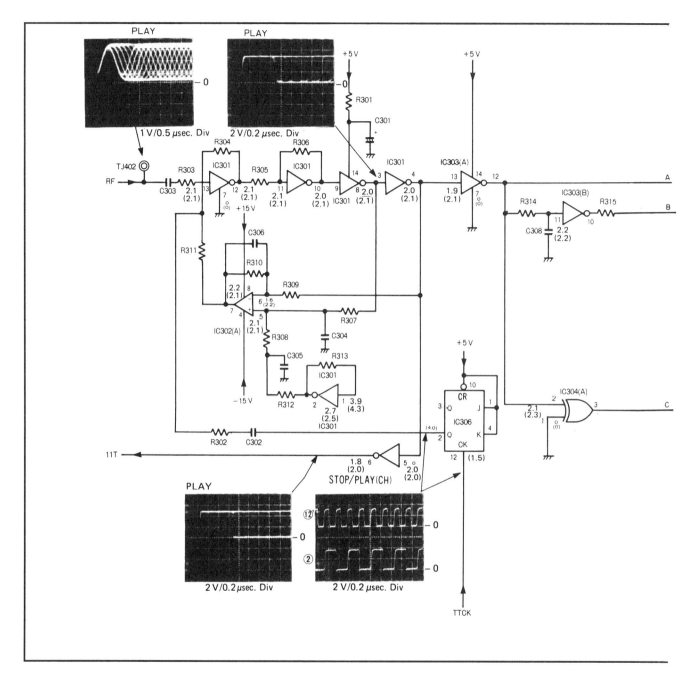

Fig. 8-3. Data and EFM extraction

pin 12. From here, it is applied to two paths, one with a delay and one with no delay. The delay circuits consist of R314, R315, C308, C309, and IC303 (segments B and C). The delay is chosen to be 0.5T, or about 0.11 microsecond. The delayed and undelayed signals are next gated by IC304 (segment B). The result is an edge signal, that is, a pulse with a width of 0.5T that occurs

whenever the RF signal rises or falls (at the edges). Refer to Fig. 8-3.

The precise pulse width of 0.5T is necessary for the proper operation of the PLL (phase-locked loop) circuit. The PLL circuit is made of phase comparator IC304 (segments C and D), integrator IC302 (segment B) and associated components, and VCO (voltage-controlled oscil-

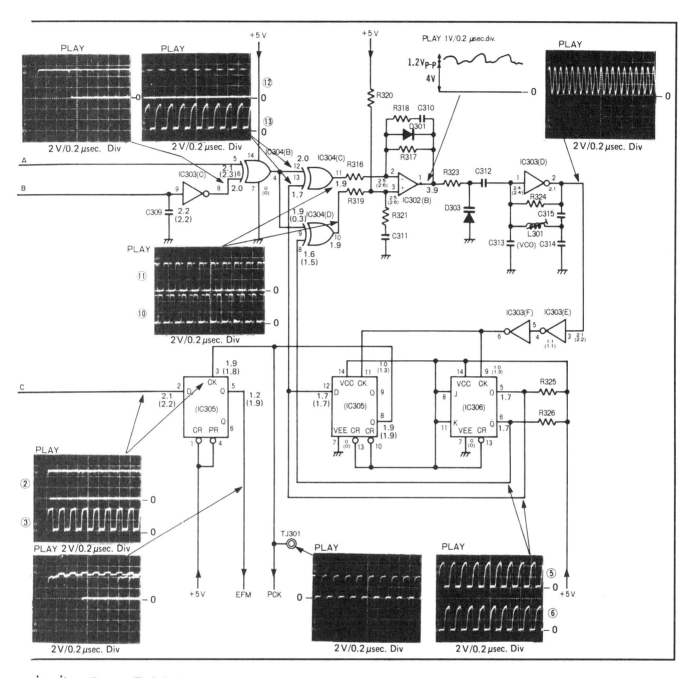

circuits. *(Courtesy Technics)*

lator) IC303 and its components. The VCO, by proper choice of L301 and C313, C314, C315, and varactor diode D303, free runs at 8.642 megahertz (twice the normal system clock). Its signal is amplified and squared by IC303 (segments E and F) and is applied to both IC306 and IC305. IC306 serves to count down the VCO signal, or divide it by 2. The inverted and noninverted outputs of IC306 from pins 6 and 5 are routed back to phase comparator stage IC304 (C and D). This is basic PLL operation. Phase comparison is made between the incoming edge signal (with 0.5T width) and the counted-down VCO signal. If a phase difference is detected, it will cause a change in the dc value to be produced by integrator IC302(B). This will affect the

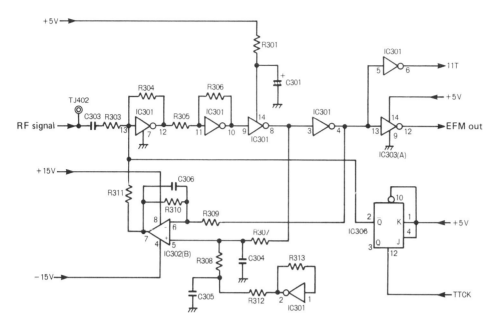

Fig. 8-4. RF signal waveshaping circuit. *(Courtesy Technics)*

frequency of the VCO by means of varactor diode D303. The frequency will change in the necessary direction to compensate for the phase difference. The VCO then is slave to (will follow) the frequency of the edge signal. We know that the edge signal, derived from the RF signal, is never at 4.321 megahertz, but it is always at *multiples* of 4.321 megahertz, and this is what the PLL is designed to be able to lock to.

The counted-down VCO signal is also applied to IC305, pin 12, and is gated out by the uncounted-down signal applied to pin 11. The precisely timed, inverted output appears at pin 8, and is known as the PCK (sometimes called playback clock, or bit clock) signal. The PCK signal is the playback bit rate clock used to decode the EFM. But in order to be sure that the edges of the playback EFM and PCK signal are coincident, they are gated by IC305. The EFM signal (from RF) is applied to pin 2 (data input) of IC305. The clock input at pin 3 is the PCK signal. The output at pin 5 is the now time-coincident EFM signal ready for decoding.

EFM DECODING

As much time and paper that was necessary to design the EFM demodulation circuitry would be necessary to fully describe it. Furthermore, some

of the details concerning the CIRC error correction scheme are guarded secrets. This means that the details of CIRC encoding are not generally available, as well as the specific methods of achieving the error correction in playback, which can differ from one manufacturer to the next. Technics' method of decoding is called Super Algorithm. Such descriptions are not for exposure. All of this is supported by the fact that the three ICs which perform EFM decoding and error correction are themselves contained on a ceramic slide, mounted vertically, and the overall pin count reduced to 45 in the Technics SL-P2. Table 8-1 lists the various duties and specifications of the three ICs MN6614F/15F/16F, which are shown in Fig. 8-5.

The basic, expected operations are performed. These include EFM demodulation, where the PCK signal is used to gate out the 14-bit EFM data words, in order to get the words with a bit pattern starting at bit 0 and ending at bit 13 (for 14-bit EFM words). Therefore, the start of frame sync must be detected, in order to know where the EFM words begin and end. The internal frame clock signal, FCLK, is generated. The synchronization signal actually extracted from the disc is called $\overline{\text{CLDCK}}$. In addition, a signal which indicates that successful EFM demodulation has been achieved is generated and is called RESY (which could be called

Table 8-1. Functions of the Main Signal-Processing ICs *(Courtesy Technics)*

	MN6614F	MN6615F	MN6616F
Main function	EFM demodulation	System timing generation	Error correction
Process	n-channel MOS 3 μm	n-channel MOS 3 μm	n-channel MOS 3 μm
Chip size	5.78 × 3.37 mm	5.64 × 5.57 mm	6.94 × 6.54 mm
Number of elements	6000	17 000	20 000
Input/output level	TTL compatible	TTL compatible	TTL compatible
Power supply	+5-V UM-1 power source	+5-V UM-1 power source	+5-V UM-1 power source
Shape	42-pin flat package	64-pin flat package	42-pin flat package

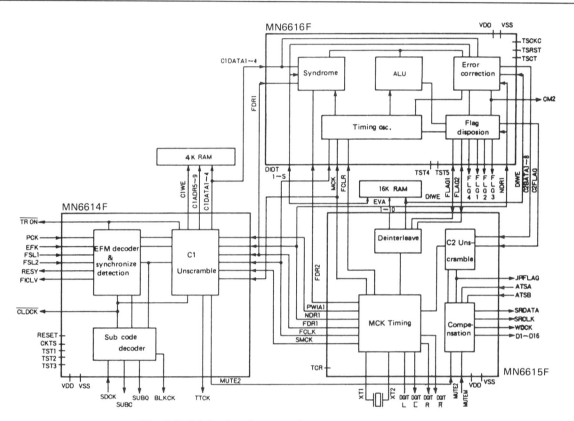

Fig. 8-5. Main signal-processing ICs. *(Courtesy Technics)*

"reliable sync"). These three signals are used in the spindle motor servo circuit.

In Fig. 8-6 the EFM demodulator IC, an MN6614F, receives the EFM signal and the PCK signal from the phase-locked loop portion of the audio playback circuits previously described. The EFM data is latched at a 14-bit rate by using the system master clock (MCK). The 14-bit EFM data is then converted back to its original 8-bit form. This IC also performs the job of unscrambling the data which was originally scrambled according to the C1 process. The C1 scrambling

was used in recording the disc, and performs a minor interleaving action. During playback this is reversed by an MN6614, and the 4K RAM, an MN2114S-3. The same memory IC can, of course, accept data and deliver data on the same four lines, by using a write enable (WE) control line. The C1 decoded data, then, appears at pins 11-14 of the 4K RAM. The subcode channel data is also decoded by the EFM demodulator IC. Remember, these eight channels of specialized data contain the Q channel, that channel which has the TOC and the continuous update

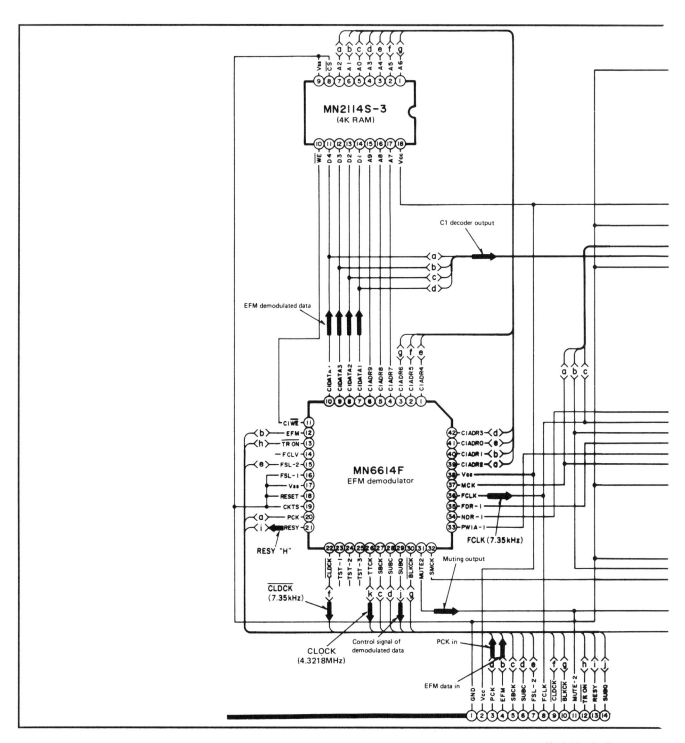

Fig. 8-6. Detailed block diagram of

information. The composite subcode signal is decoded and appears at the connector IC, pin 6. The separated Q channel data appears at connector IC pin 14. The Q channel data is used by the system control IC401 for display purposes, and programming.

Three signals used by the spindle motor servo are also generated by the EFM demodulator. The FCLK signal, the data derived frame sync signal, and the $\overline{\text{CLDCK}}$, the crystal reference frame rate sync signal, are both used for the CLV (constant linear velocity) servo. RESY,

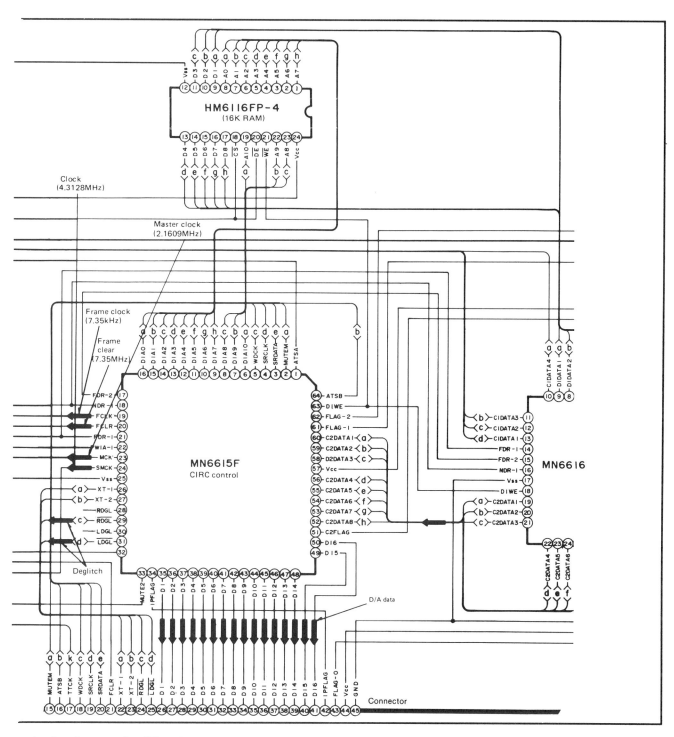

main signal-processing ICs. *(Courtesy Technics)*

which initiates the CLV servo, is also generated, appearing at pin 13 of the connector.

The CIRC controller IC, an MN6615F, performs the duties of developing the system timing signals, C2 unscrambling, deinterleaving, and interpolation. This IC runs off of the master crystal clock, generated by crystal X701, con-

nected to the connector at pins 22 and 23. The internal master clock (MCK) is generated, and runs at a frequency of 2.16 megahertz. Deinterleaving is the reverse of the interleaving process used when a CD is recorded. The deinterleaving process requires various delay times, some many frames long. To achieve these delays, another

RAM IC is used, an HM6616. The CIRC controller determines when to write and read the 8-bit data to/from the RAM IC. C2 unscrambling is performed, as well as the interpolation process. Interpolation is the "guessing" of what a missing bit, or bits, should be by examining the adjacent bits. Should a large playback error occur, where both the P and Q parity words cannot provide correction, interpolation is performed. Although the action of interpolation can actually cause a form of distortion (since a guessed value is used, not the actual value), it is used rather infrequently. Even so, the distortion caused by interpolation is far less than when the interpolation is not used to cover the missing bits.

The CIRC controller is the IC which delivers the 16-bit digital audio samples, reconstructed from the 8-bit form. These data lines, D1 through D14, are available at LSI module pins 26-41. The left deglitch ($\overline{\text{LDGL}}$) and right deglitch ($\overline{\text{RDGL}}$) signals are generated by the CIRC controller, and their use will be evident later.

The error-correction IC, an MN6616 in Fig. 8-5, performs both levels of error correction, the P level (P parity word) and the Q level (Q parity word). Errors detected at the P level are performed after the C1 descramble process and are flagged by this IC so that they can be corrected. Correction is done by a combination effort of this IC and CIRC controller. A similar action occurs when the Q parity level detects an error, except that it is done just after deinterleaving. Beyond this, the interpolation will be evoked.

As was mentioned, most of these operations are not easily viewable since the circuit board is mounted vertically. Just remember that the most important signals coming from the board are the 16-bit-wide digital audio samples, the decoded subcode channels, and system timing signals and control signals used in the servo circuits.

DIGITAL-TO-ANALOG CONVERSION

The 16-bit-wide digital audio samples are fed to IC801, the digital-to-analog converter, at pins 1 through 16 (refer to Fig. 8-7). Quite simply, the composite, serialized audio stream is output from pin 17. Remember that during the recording of the CD, the separate left and right audio signals were sampled, and then converted to serial format. This means that one of the simultaneously occurring samples has to be delayed so that it can fit behind the other sample, that is, in serial format. To split the serial audio stream into two separate left and right channels, two switches operating at the speed of the sample clock (44.1 kilohertz) will alternately pass or block the serial signal into two paths. Two switching signals are used to accomplish this; the $\overline{\text{RDGL}}$, and $\overline{\text{LDGL}}$ (right and left deglitch) signals from the LSI module are used. For the left channel, the $\overline{\text{LDGL}}$ signal operates the switch, IC802. The right channel path uses the $\overline{\text{RDGL}}$ signal to operate the switch, IC805. When the left channel is allowed to pass the audio signal, the right channel is blocking. Conversely, when the right channel is passing the audio signal, the left channel is blocking. This action performs a kind of serial-to-parallel conversion, as all the signals intended for the left channel will be passed by the left deglitching action. All the intended right channel information is directed through the right deglitching circuit. To remove any 44.1-kilohertz switching noise from the audio signals, the latter are low-pass filtered to a frequency of about 20 kilohertz. The left channel filter is LPF801, and LPF802 is for the right channel. The playback response curve can be altered by the combination of C805 and R805, which are connected off of pin 5 of LPF801. For the right channel the same action can occur due to C811 and R817 at LPF802. Compact discs may be recorded with an emphasis, or high-frequency boost. Currently most are not, but if this option is taken, the deemphasis must be done in playback. Deemphasis is under the control of the EMPH (emphasis) signal from the system control, IC401. When deemphasis is required, EMPH goes high and closes another switch inside IC802 (left channel) and IC805 (right channel). This action will shunt resistors R805 and R817, respectively, to achieve the necessary action.

There is at this point a difference between the left and right channels. There is a delay of one-half the sampling clock cycle between channels. This delay was intentionally put in during recording so that samples could be serialized, one placed after the other. A delay of about 11 microseconds (a period of half the sampling frequency) is needed for this. On playback and deglitching, this phase difference still exists. If it is not compensated, it could change the stereo image at the higher frequencies. To correct this, the left channel is delayed by 11 microseconds by IC803 and IC804(A) and their associated components. Fig. 8-7 shows the phase delay which is still apparent right after the low-pass filters. Once it is phase corrected, the left channel signal is applied to drive IC804(B). The right channel driver is IC806. From the drivers the two audio channels will, in most cases, be sent to the output terminals, but this path can be broken through the action of relay RLY801. This relay operates during the mute mode (at start-up and in large errors) and will ground the terminals to achieve the muting effect.

THE FOCUS SERVO

The difference signal from the photodiode pairs is converted from a current signal to a voltage signal inside IC103 at pins 13 and 14, as in Fig. 8-8. There is a balance adjustment, VR102, to equalize the output of these two stages. The equalized difference signal is amplified and viewable out of pin 17, at test point TJ101. At this point, external to the IC, the two main focus adjustments are connected. Focus gain, VR101, adjusts the amplitude of the difference signal, which will determine how far the lens will be driven for focus error correction. For too low an amplitude, the lens will not do its job properly. For too large a signal, the lens will hunt, or rebound because of its spring suspension. The focus offset control, VR103, applies a dc voltage from a bipolar divider (from −5 volts to +5 volts). This serves to place the lens position in the center of its permitted travel, to allow for the maximum focus correction capability. The offset control will electrically compensate for any dc offset from the difference amplifier (at pin 17) itself and for minor differences in the suspension of the focus lens from optical assembly to optical assembly.

Under normal playback, this difference signal, now the total focus error signal, FE, will be sent to a switch located inside IC103, at pin 18. The FE signal, under normal playback, will go to the FE amplifiers, made of IC105 (A and B). These in turn will operate the high-current drivers, Q107 and Q108. These transistors form a bipolar drive, which is capable of moving the lens above and below its normal physical resting point. When the disc is first started, that is, when play is first initiated, an initial state of focus must also be achieved. Strictly speaking, the focusing lens is driven above and below its resting point just to see if a disc is indeed present. This is not considered normal playback, it is start-up. A low-frequency oscillator, internal to IC103 at pins 27 and 28 produces a 2-hertz square wave, visible at pin 28. It is converted into a triangular waveform at pin 26. At start-up, a special signal from the system control microprocessor, IC401, called FO ON (active low) is applied to IC103, pin 2. This switches the path for the 2-hertz focus search oscillator through to pin 26, and then drives the lens. When RF is detected, IC401 will disable this focus search effort, and the system switches to FE focus control.

These sequences can be summed up in the timing chart of Fig. 8-9. Waveform A is the focus search triangular wave at pin 26 of IC103 (of which only the rising portion is seen). As the lens moves from its resting point, it will come within a focusing range, if a disc is present. First it will go through too-near focus, in focus, and then too-far focus. The elliptical patterns produce waveform B, the focus error signal. Here, in focus search, it takes the form of the so-called S-curve, where the rising (positive) portion represents too-near focus. As the S-curve goes toward zero, it indicates that proper focus is achieved. When the lens is driven for a too-far focus condition, the negative hump of the S-curve results.

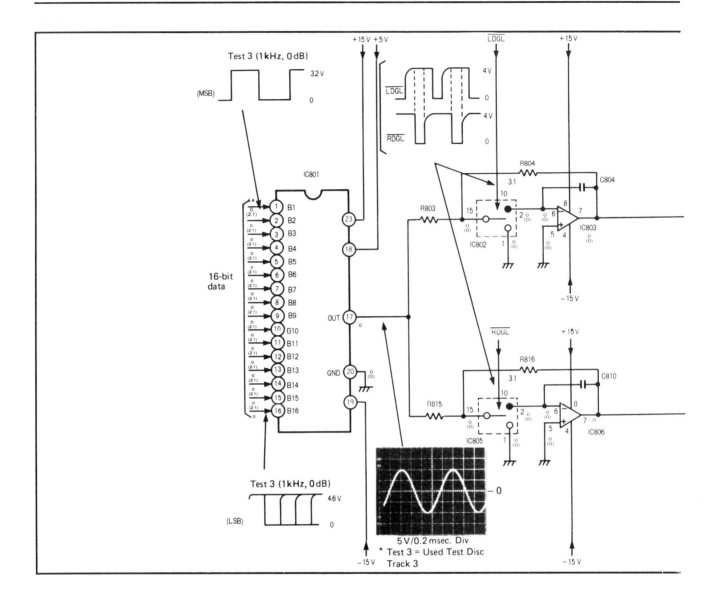

Fig. 8-7. Block diagram for

The S-curve is gated within the comparator stage of IC103, and produces waveform C. Waveform C is differentiated to become waveform D. Resistor R126 and capacitor C119, at pin 24, form a time-constant circuit, which yields waveform E. Ideally, if RF is to be detected, it will be detected within this time period; if not, the circuit must wait for the next focus search cycle.

Waveform F shows the actual RF data recovery, as the focus lens searches. The rising edge of waveform D switches the servo loop over to FE, instead of search. This is the action depicted in waveform H. Waveform G is the RF detection delayed signal.

THE TRACKING SERVO

This servo system is not quite as simple as the focus or spindle motor servo, primarily because there are really two separate but related driven elements. The fine tracking control, which can perform accurate tracking in a range of about ±40 tracks (80 tracks total) is usually the system referred to as the tracking servo. After 80 tracks have passed, and this servo can no longer play the track it should, the entire optical assembly, which is driven by a lead screw and motor, will move into the next 80-track segment. This servo action is, in the case of Technics, referred to as traverse motor servo.

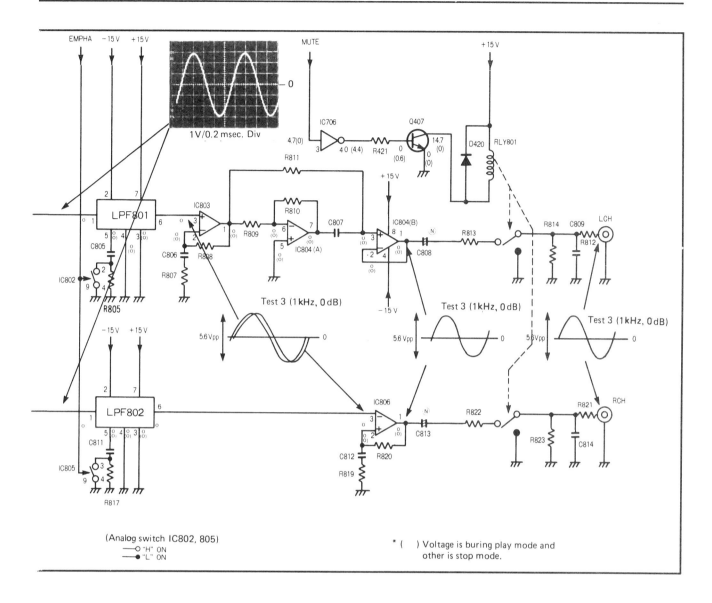

D/A conversion. *(Courtesy Technics)*

Fig. 8-10 shows a partially disassembled optical assembly, and it is evident that it rides on tubular rails. The optical assembly consists of the enclosed laser optics with the printed-circuit boards for the laser diode and the photodiodes for pickup. The focus lens is mounted in a suspended coil assembly resembling a speaker voice coil. And, like a speaker voice coil, it is suspended in a magnetic field supplied by several permanent magnets. The largest of the coils, which is wrapped around a plastic frame, is the focus coil, and it provides vertical movement for focus. The two smaller pairs of coils, mounted on both narrow ends of the frame, are the tracking coils. These provide lateral movement of the focus lens, for tracking. The traverse motor is pulsed, during normal playback, as the voltage driving the tracking coils starts to increase past a preset threshold. This makes sense, as the voltage driving the tracking coils is a direct indication of how far the lens has shifted in an effort to stay on track.

During normal playback, the two offset tracking photodiodes (the SL-P2 is a three-beam system) are used to determine tracking. In Fig. 8-11 the two photodiode segment outputs are applied to IC104 pins 11 and 12. Inside the IC is what amounts to a differential amplifier. The photodiode segment which has the larger amplitude will provide the signal to exit the stage.

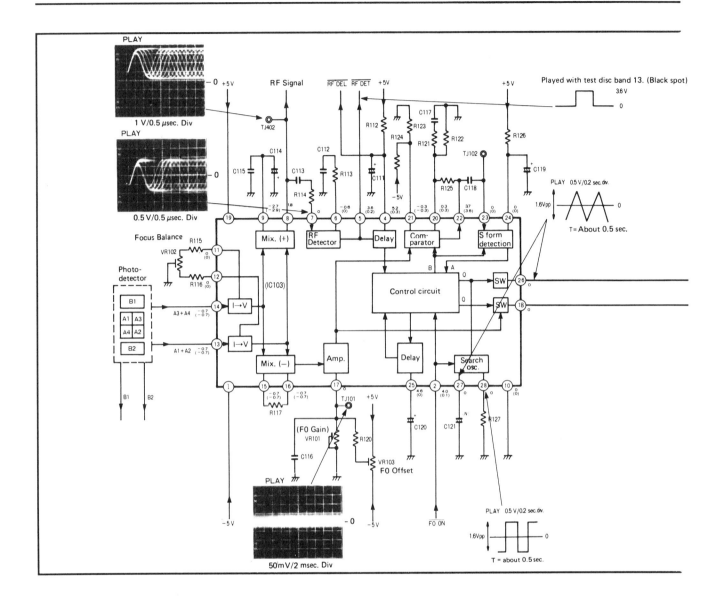

Fig. 8-8. Simplified schematic diagram

The tracking balance control, VR105, connected to pins 14 and 16, adjusts for any sensitivity difference between photodiodes, by controlling the gain of the amplification stages inside IC104. The tracking error signal, TE, is visible at pin 4, which is also test point TJ103. The error signal gain and offset (dc level) are adjustable via VR104 and VR106, respectively, and are similar in function to the gain and offset controls used in the focus servo. The TE signal is sent through a switching stage inside the IC, however, before appearing at pin 9. The switch is used to block the TE signal in the case of search or skip. Search or skip is not normal playback, and the tracking servo is not allowed to try to adapt to the rapidly moving optics. The controlling signal for the switch is a signal called $\overline{\text{TR ON}}$, for "tracking on." From system control IC401, this signal goes low for normal tracking, and changes between low and high for the case of search and skip. The TE signal, whether allowed to be switched to pin 9 or not, is also applied to a comparator inside the IC which is used to sense the extremes of the signal as it rises and falls sharply. Such sharp rises and falls are only seen in the case of search or skip, and are caused by the two tracking photodiode segments going through minimum and maximum outputs as the optics move (remember, only in the search or skip modes).

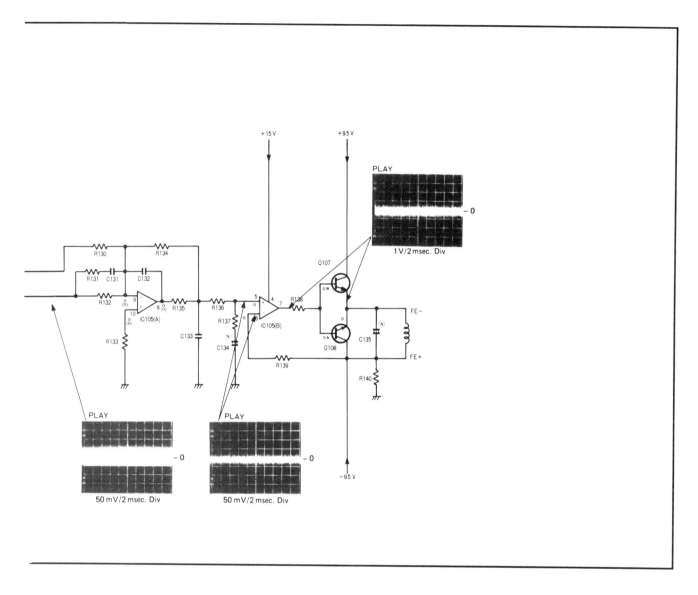

of the focus servo circuit. *(Courtesy Technics)*

During normal playback, TE doesn't rise or fall in the same way as it does for search or skip, and in fact resembles the RF data (understandably so, since it comes from the same pits). The photograph at pin 9 of IC104 in Fig. 8-11 shows the TE signal for normal play. The comparator essentially squares up the TE signal, which is output at pin 5 and is called the CROSS signal. This CROSS signal is used to indicate that a track has been jumped, or crossed. The CROSS signal is further shaped by Q403 and IC403. This signal, from IC403 pin 1, is called the track count, or TCNT, signal, and is used by the system control, IC401. The TCNT signal is sent to system control IC401 and is utilized during the

search mode to indicate that the optics are skipping over the tracks.

The TE signal from pin 9 of IC104 is low frequency boosted by IC105(C) and its components. There is a dc component to the TE signal that is associated with the lens requiring more and more tracking drive to stay on course. The TE signal is next either passed through or blocked by FET Q105. Capacitor C173 will store the last instant of the TE signal in the case of Q105 being turned off, blocking the TE signal. This switching action is controlled by the THOLD signal from the system control, IC401. This tracking hold signal, sent through Q404 and Q106, is used during the jumping of tracks.

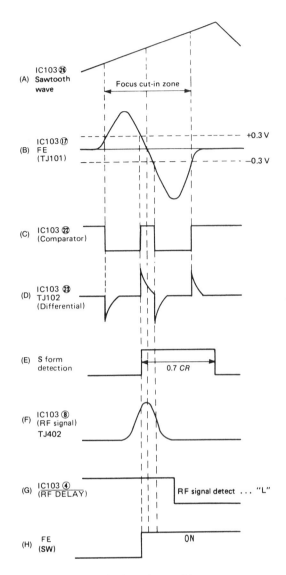

Fig. 8-9. Timing chart of focus servo.
(Courtesy Technics)

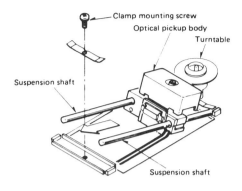

(A) Assembly mounted on rails.

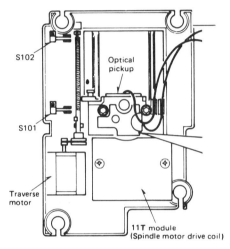

(B) Traverse motor and lead screw.

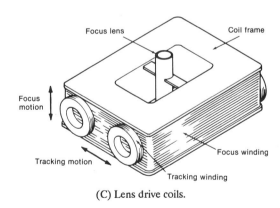

(C) Lens drive coils.

Fig. 8-10. Optical assembly *(Courtesy Technics)*

Jumping is performed when search is enacted, such as manually pressing the search forward or search reverse button. THOLD turns off Q105, and the high resistance of the FET will keep the charge on C173 stored. Under normal playback conditions, the TE signal does pass through Q105 and is applied to the driver circuit made of IC105(D), Q109, and Q110. Q109 and Q110 form a bipolar drive for the tracking coil. A negative-feedback loop through R180 to pin 2 of IC105 stabilizes the drive.

Track jumping is accomplished by two signals called KICK F (forward) and KICK R (reverse), issued from the system control, IC401.

The KICK pulses are issued when search is activated. When the consumer chooses to search forward, he or she presses the search forward button and, even if it is pressed very briefly, the lens does advance. During this jump the TE signal is held by THOLD, so that after it jumps, the lens will assume the previous TE voltage and be much more likely to recover with no problems. Similarly, the $\overline{\text{TR ON}}$ signal turns off the switch inside IC104, so that the gross error voltage that occurs when track jump occurs will not upset the normal function of IC105(C), and therefore the charge on C173. The KICK F pulse is applied to pin 2 of IC201 (one stage), and the KICK R pulse is applied to pin 3. When searching forward once, the KICK F pulse will be sent to IC105(D) pin 2, and then to the bipolar drivers Q109 and Q110. This pulse will shift the lens in the forward direction until the CROSS signal sent to IC401 indicates that a jump occurred. At this point, system control IC401 will issue the KICK R pulse to cancel the movement of the lens (Fig. 8-12).

The opposite action occurs when searching backward. First, the KICK R pulse is issued to get the lens to shift back toward the center of the disc. When the CROSS signal changes state, the lens movement is cancelled by the KICK F pulse. When the search mode is released, the $\overline{\text{TR ON}}$ signal again goes low, and the $\overline{\text{THOLD}}$ signal will go high. This permits the previous error voltage to now drive the lens, and restores the operation of obtaining the TE signal.

THE TRAVERSE SERVO

There is one more section of the tracking servo circuit that should be examined and that is the generation of the traverse error signal, called TRVE. This is actually a sample of the lens driving signal which is used to determine if it is time to move the traverse motor, as is done gently and repeatedly during play and certainly during search. It was mentioned briefly that as the optical assembly sits still, the focus lens must continuously shift to stay on track. For the lens to shift in this way a continually changing voltage is necessary to drive it. In the normal play mode the drive voltage will continually decrease (below 0 volts). When the voltage has dropped far enough, system control IC401 issues a pulse to advance the traverse motor. When searching in reverse, the driving voltage will increase above zero, a

point where IC401 knows to turn the traverse motor in reverse. Refer to Fig. 8-13.

The lens tracking coil signal is sent not only to the coil but through R205. The combination of R205 and C201 forms a low-pass filter which removes the high-frequency TE information, so that mainly just a changing dc level remains. This signal is sent to a differential amplifier made of Q201 and Q202. The TRVE signal is taken from the collector of Q202. This TRVE signal is shifted positive by the action of the differential amplifier. The TRVE signal is applied to system control IC401, at pin 22, in Fig. 8-13. If the TRVE signal starts to drop too far, the IC will issue a FWD pulse to advance the traverse motor (see Fig. 8-14). The FWD command comes from pin 28 of the IC and is integrated by R213 and C203. This is then applied to IC201 (one stage) where a sawtooth waveform is visible. From here it will operate bipolar drivers Q203 and Q204. During normal play a sawtooth waveform with a slight positive dc level is applied to the motor. When the sawtooth peaks, the motor will turn gently to advance the lead screw, which in turn will smoothly advance the optics. But, when the system is searching in reverse, the lens will continually kick in reverse, increasing the TRVE signal. Once this signal is past a set threshold, IC401 will issue a REV command. This pulse is not integrated like the FWD pulse is, and turns the motor somewhat more abruptly, but in reverse in order to achieve reverse search. During the pause mode in playback the FWD command is not issued and the traverse motor won't advance. As might be expected, the lens tracking servo is also in a state of hold. This is necessary because the TE signal will contain large errors as a false jump signal is generated. (This is called a false jump since it is the relative movement of the tracks against a stationary lens which causes the same effect as a jump.)

THE MOTOR SPINDLE SERVO

The compact disc system is designed around a disc that runs at a constant *linear* velocity (CLV).

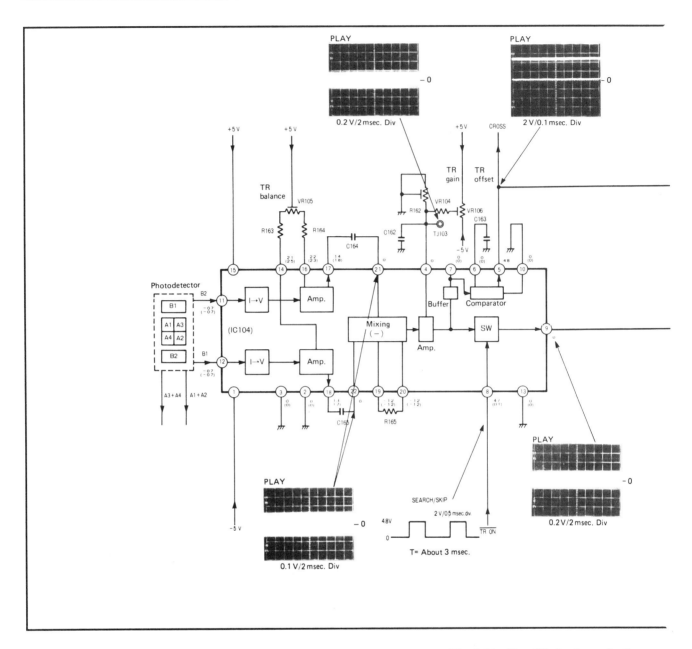

Fig. 8-11. Simplified schematic diagram

Conventional records (LPs, 45s) run at a constant *angular* velocity (CAV). In CAV systems the disc spins at a speed such as 33⅓ revolutions per minute, and nothing more. What's important to realize is that when a stylus plays the first selection of an LP, more vinyl passes the diamond tip per revolution than at the inner grooves, or the last song. And since the revolutions per minute speed is constant, it is the velocity which is greater at the first song and steadily decreases through the last selection. This

fact creates a compromise in CAV systems, since the writing speed, and therefore fidelity of the recording, is better at the outermost grooves, and steadily degrades toward the inner grooves. The advantage to CAV systems is that their speed (in revolutions per minute) is very easy to regulate.

The compact disc uses CLV instead. It is desirable to have the same writing speed (velocity) throughout the disc. This will enable the construction of uniform pits and flats. In other words, in a CLV system like CD, a 3*T* pit/

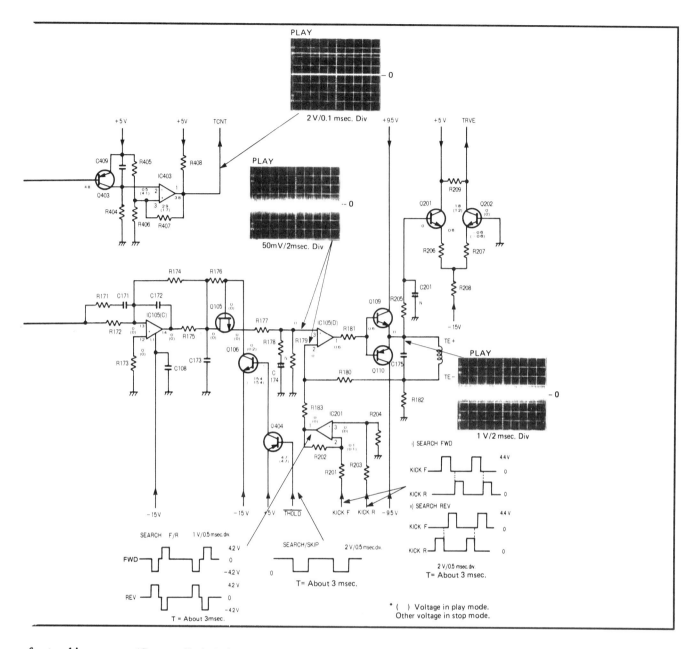

for tracking servo. *(Courtesy Technics)*

flat sequence at the innermost grooves of the disc will occupy the exact amount of space as a 3T sequence at the outermost grooves. The sizes of the pits and flats are the same at all portions of the disc. In this manner the optics can operate within a specified frequency range. Conversely, if the CD system used CAV, the dimensions of the pits and flats would continually change from the beginning to the ending of the disc. At the innermost grooves, or beginning of the CD, the optics would have to read pits and flats which are

smaller for a given period (let's say 3T) than at the ending of the disc. Therefore the optics would have to be sensitive to a higher-frequency range compared with CLV. This, then, would raise the price of the optics. It is more desirable to incorporate a CLV servo system, in order to keep the difficulty of manufacturing down, as well as the price.

At the beginning of the disc, where the table of contents (TOC) is recorded, the disc spins at about 500 revolutions per minute. At the

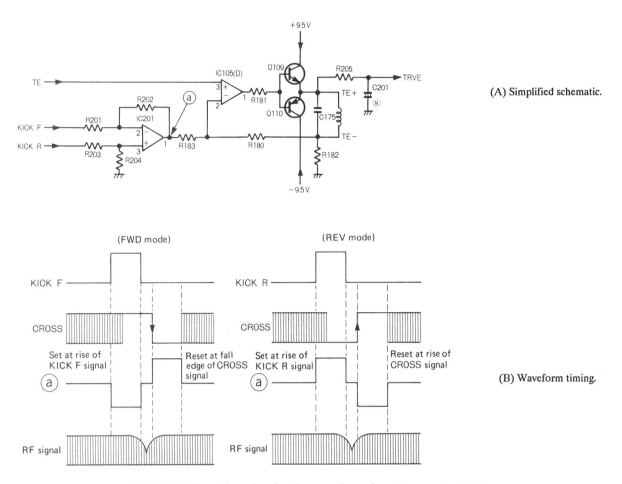

(A) Simplified schematic.

(B) Waveform timing.

Fig. 8-12. Track jumping for the search mode. *(Courtesy Technics)*

outermost periphery, near the end of a 72-minute disc, the speed drops to about 200 revolutions per minute. This is very visible to most owners of CD players. The criteria for determining the proper disc speed are not as simple as one might guess. During play, the frame synchronizing words in the EFM data stream are used to regulate the playback disc speed. This makes sense, because it is known that the frequency of the frame sync words should be 7.35 kilohertz. A simple phase-locked loop circuit can be used to achieve this. But there are also the conditions of starting the disc from the stop mode and search to contend with.

There are, then, three stages of spindle motor servo control:

1. Constant rotation (this is start-up).

2. 11T (this is coarse servo control).

3. CLV (this is fine servo control).

The block diagram in Fig. 8-15 shows in simple form how this system works. The three servo stages are shown. The 11T and CLV circuits are applied to a logic switching stage, which will select one or the other's error signal. The constant rotation servo is controlled from a signal from system control IC401, called ACC (motor acceleration). This is the servo loop that will be discussed first.

Looking at the overall spindle servo schematic in Fig. 8-16, we can isolate IC501 (motor drive) and IC505(C) (inverter for ACC). When the play command is given, the turntable-on signal, $\overline{\text{TT ON}}$, goes low. This signal, a master on/off control for the spindle motor (sometimes called turntable, TT) comes from the system control, IC401. Also, since this is start-up, the ACC signal is also issued to get the motor up to a nominal speed quickly.

Now concentrate on the partial schematic in Fig. 8-17. The $\overline{\text{TT ON}}$ active-low signal is in-

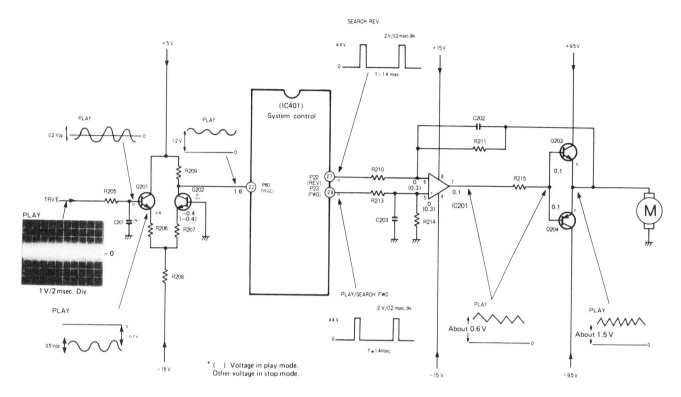

Fig. 8-13. Simplified schematic for traverse servo. *(Courtesy Technics)*

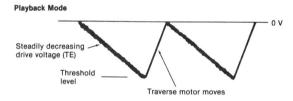

Fig. 8-14. Normal operation of the traverse servo.
(Courtesy Technics)

verted by IC505(A) and the high is applied to IC501 pin 2. The inverted ACC signal is applied to pin 11 of the same IC. This input, at pin 11, is the servo error voltage input to IC501 in all cases. These actions start the spindle motor running, without regard to the actual fine-control speed. This mode of operation is very short in duration, and lasts only long enough for the optics to detect not only a reflection from the disc, but some assemblance of RF data. The first action, though, is that of spinning the motor, which can be demonstrated by placing a disc in the player upside down and then pressing PLAY. The unit will spin the disc, but on failure to extract any data it will stop. In the normal case however, some RF data will be detected, and this

indicates the presence of a disc, and then the need to go to a finer mode of spindle servo control.

It is also important to note here, that during the condition of skip (in addition to start-up) the constant-rotation loop is selected. When the unit is in access (skip mode) the optics must travel to the selected track quickly, and the constant rotational servo, because it doesn't require the action of a true phase-locked loop, allows for this.

Once RF data is detected, a condition easily known from the signal RF DET, from IC103, is used to switch the spindle motor servo from constant rotational speed to the 11T servo, the rough or course servo control loop. The name 11T is derived from the longest length of a pit or flat allowed, that of 10 zeros and a one, or 11 clock cycles ($11T$). This pattern is guaranteed to occur once per frame, because it is a part of the frame sync word. The 11T servo loop is built around this time period of $11T$ (4.321 megahertz/11 = 196 kilohertz), and looks at how a capacitor charges with respect to this known rate.

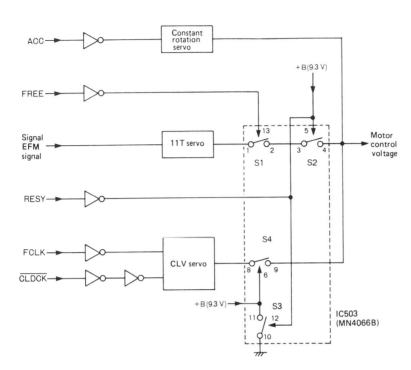

Fig. 8-15. Simplified block diagram for spindle motor servo. *(Courtesy Technics)*

Look at the partial schematic for the 11T servo loop circuit in Fig. 8-18. First, the $\overline{\text{RF DET}}$ active-low signal is applied to Q504. When this signal goes low for RF detection, Q504 will be turned off, thus no longer shunting the 11T error signal developed at the collector of Q503. The error signal at the emitter of Q503 is developed by Q501 and Q502 and their associated circuitry. The input to Q501 is the playback RF data, previously squared up. If Q501 is off, C508 will start to charge through R504, R505 and VR501, the 11T adjustment. Since the frame sync word contains one sequence of 11*T* in which the EFM signal will be high, the charging of C508 is controlled. Naturally, EFM transitions less than the 11*T* period will also discharge C508. What's important is that C508 can charge no higher than that level allowed by a period of 11*T*. This voltage is applied to one of the amplifier stages inside of IC502, at pin 5. Coming out from pin 7, it continues to the other amplifier stage in IC502, and is output at pin 1. This output is switch selected by one stage of IC503(A). When the input to pin 13 of IC503 goes high, the switch will close, and send the speed error voltage forward in the path. The next switch in that path

is IC503(B), controlled by the signal RESY from system control IC401.

Now look at the timing chart for servo switch selection in Fig. 8-19 and also refer to some of the previous diagrams. From STOP, the spindle motor will accelerate, due to the application of the ACC signal from the system control microprocessor. After a short period the ACC signal goes low, so that it does not contribute to the motor drive. At the same time, the FREE signal (free-run) from the system control microprocessor goes high. When FREE goes high, it opens switch 1, that is, IC503(A). This will block the 11T servo error voltage, and the motor will free run (coast) for a brief period. When the FREE signal goes low, switch IC503(A) closes. The RESY signal, still low, applies a high to pin 5 of IC503 (stage B), so that it too closes, and passes the 11T servo error voltage to pin 11 of IC501, the drive IC.

Looking back at the $\overline{\text{RF DET}}$ signal in Fig. 8-18, remember that it grounded the charging capacitor (11*T* period) before going into IC502, pin 5. If, in the event of dropout during playback, this signal will momentarily go high, which will again block the error voltage from entering

IC502. This is done to prevent a gross error from a highly charged C508 from upsetting the rest of the circuit. At the same time, Q505 will also be turned on, and this will ground the voltage at pin 13 of IC503, thus opening this switch. This action shuts off the 11T loop during a large dropout. Also notice Q655, whose base is connected through R665 to the output of IC502 at pin 7. If the voltage at pin 7 goes too high, it will forward bias Q655. This will allow the input to the amplifier, pin 5 of IC502, to be grounded. The emitter of Q655 is connected to the BRAKE (turntable stop command) line from system control IC401. Under the normal running condition, the BRAKE signal is low, and Q655's emitter has a complete path. When the BRAKE command is given (turntable stop command), Q655 can no longer shunt any error signal to ground. The role of Q655, then, is to keep the spindle motor speed from getting too low, which would cause the level of pin 7 of IC502 to go higher. During the braking action when the spindle motor stops, the level will be sufficient to trigger the amplifier shown as IC403 to switch states. That is, the level of pin 6 of IC403 will exceed the level at pin 5 (set by R509, R510) and the output at pin 7 will go low. This is called the $\overline{\text{TT STOP}}$ (turntable stop) signal, which is active low, and sent to the system control microprocessor to indicate that the turntable has stopped. According to the servo switching timing chart, Fig. 8-19, when the RESY signal goes high, the system will switch to the CLV servo loop.

After the 11T servo has been in control for a short time, not only will RF be detected, but it will be able to be decoded, that is, the EFM data stream will be extractable. Upon this, the RESY signal from the LSI module will turn off the 11T loop. Fig. 8-20 shows the partial schematic for the CLV loop. Because EFM data has been successfully decoded, a frame rate signal called $\overline{\text{CLDCK}}$ from the LSI module will be available. The $\overline{\text{CLDCK}}$ signal is applied to two back-to-back inverter stages shown as IC706 (pin 13) and IC505 (pin 6). At the same time the signal called FCLK (frame clock), derived from the crystal oscillator for the LSI module, is applied to an inverter stage, IC505 (pin 7). The FCLK and $\overline{\text{CLDCK}}$ signal are phase compared by the four gates of IC504. The two outputs from the gates are combined through R522 and R523 to become the total error voltage. The error signal is filtered by R520, R521, C511, and C512. When the LSI module makes the RESY signal go high, it will cause switch S3 of IC503(C) to open, thus causing pin 6 of IC503(D) (switch S4) to go high. This closes S4 and passes the filtered CLV error voltage to pin 11 of IC501.

In summary, the constant rotational speed loop is under control of the ACC signal only; it is not switched as the other two loops are. The 11T loop is based on the longest pit/flat sequence that can occur in the EFM process, and does occur, in the frame sync word. The fine-control CLV servo action is determined by the phase difference between the playback frame clock, $\overline{\text{CLDCK}}$, and the counted-down crystal reference, FCLK.

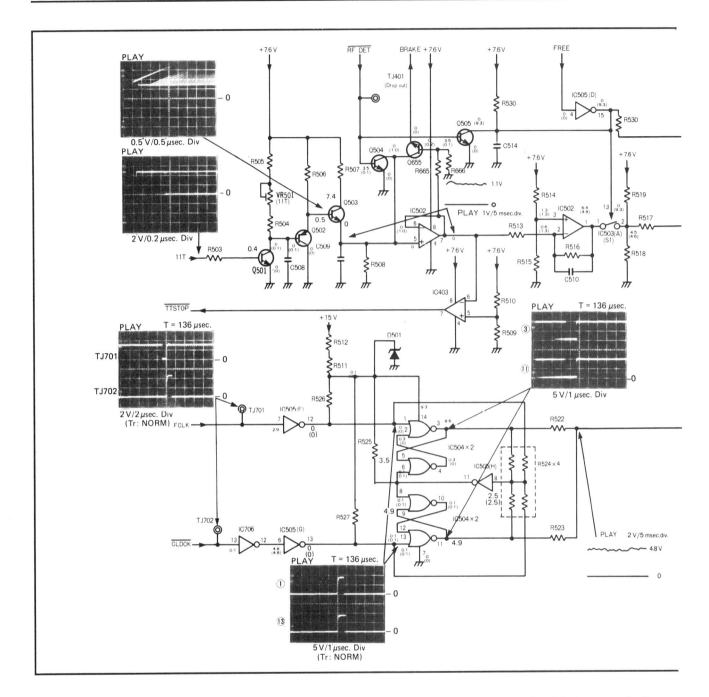

Fig. 8-16. Simplified schematic diagram

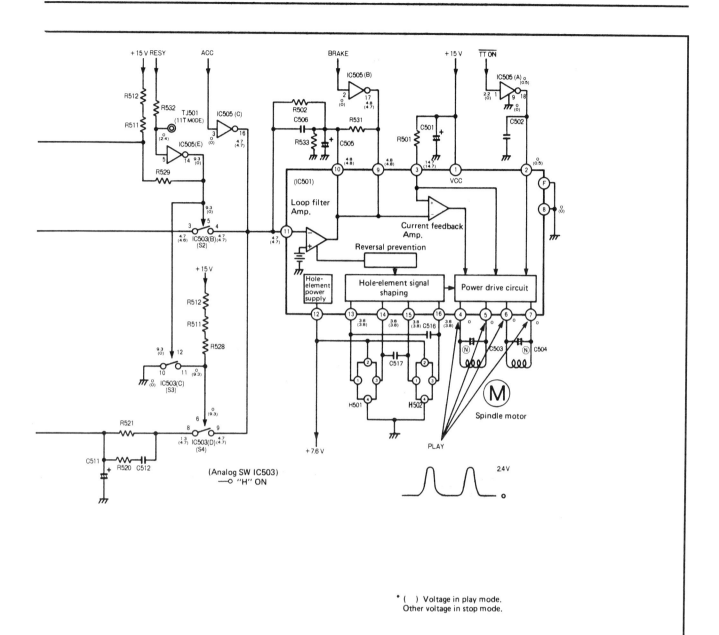

* ( ) Voltage in play mode.
Other voltage in stop mode.

for spindle motor servo. *(Courtesy Technics)*

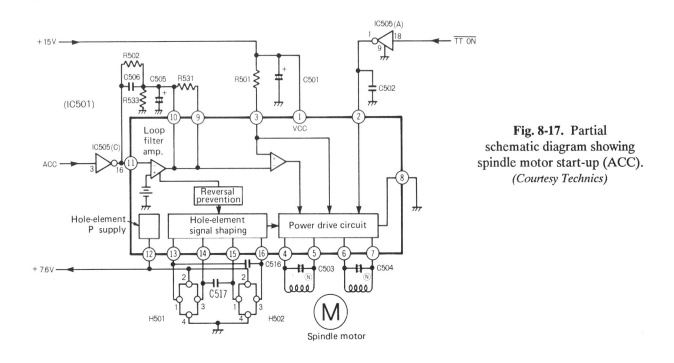

Fig. 8-17. Partial schematic diagram showing spindle motor start-up (ACC). *(Courtesy Technics)*

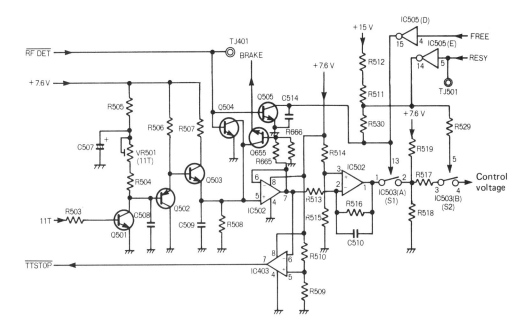

Fig. 8-18. Partial schematic diagram for spindle motor 11T servo. *(Courtesy Technics)*

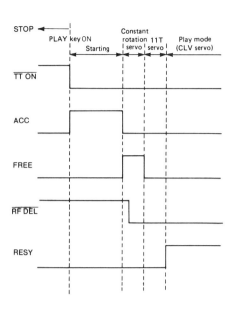

Fig. 8-19. Timing chart for spindle motor servo selection. *(Courtesy Technics)*

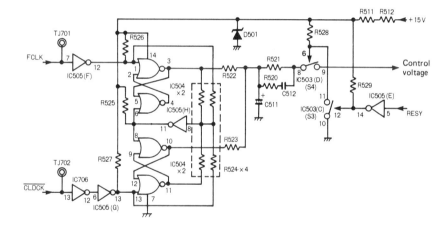

Fig. 8-20. Partial schematic for spindle motor servo, showing the CLV circuit. *(Courtesy Technics)*

Circuit Descriptions, Part 2

In this section we will deal with that circuitry responsible for the overall control of the player, and that is the system control circuit. As in any other high-technology product, for example a VCR or late-model television set, the entire device, in this case a CD player, is controlled by a microprocessor. Perhaps the single most important reason that microprocessors are used in this way is to provide more fancy features and more user convenience. In the case of the Technics SL-P2, we find that it is a full-featured device, complete with a program display, programmability, remote control, feather-touch buttons, etc. It is these, the now "expected," features that demand the use of a microprocessor.

SYSTEM CONTROL CIRCUITS

For the SL-P2, the simplified block diagram of the system control circuits is shown in Fig. 9-1. The system microprocessor, IC401 (an MN15844), is common to all the subblocks in the diagram. We see that the LSI module sends status information to IC401. In addition to the focus and tracking servos the traverse servo takes

commands from IC401. System sensors, such as the door open/close switches, the optical assembly position sensors, and the rest and end switches, all provide input to the microprocessor for machine status. The command to run the loading motor, either for door open or door close, comes from system control. The fluorescent display is controlled totally by the microprocessor, as are the front-panel buttons. The first part to be examined, then, will be the operation of the front-panel push buttons, more often called the *key matrix* circuit.

KEY MATRIX CIRCUIT

Look at the key matrix diagram shown in Fig. 9-2. The term key matrix simply refers to the push buttons as keys, and that the method of wiring them for detection by the microprocessor is that of a matrix. There are 25 front-panel buttons and internal switches which the microprocessor monitors. There aren't 25 different inputs, however, to the microprocessor; there are really just four, shown as pins 29, 30, 31, 32. The microprocessor also produces nine key matrix

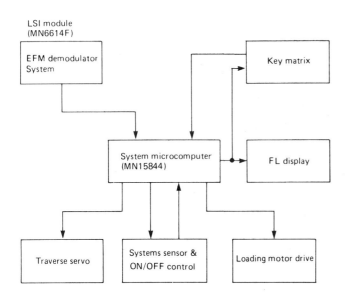

Fig. 9-1. Basic block diagram of the system control. *(Courtesy Technics)*

nine key matrix outputs are also used to create the front-panel display. The microprocessor in effect scans the nine outputs. That is, it produces a high at just one output at a time, and rapidly sequences through the nine of them. The microprocessor will know which program to execute, depending on which of the nine outputs appears at a specific input. For example, if the play button (S602) is pressed, it will tie output line D0 (pin 51) to input line P31 (pin 30). The microprocessor is a custom IC whose internal program recognizes this as the play command, and it will perform the operations of starting the spindle motor, focus search, tracking servo, etc., if the door is closed. If the door is not closed, it will have to be closed and then the play operations will begin. Each of the nine output lines uses diodes to isolate the input lines. The output lines are not always at a logic high, and if a button is pressed when its line is low, before a scan pulse comes, the diodes will prevent any backward loading of the output lines.

outputs, and it is the various combinations of the outputs being tied to the inputs which will make up the 25 conditions necessary to monitor. The

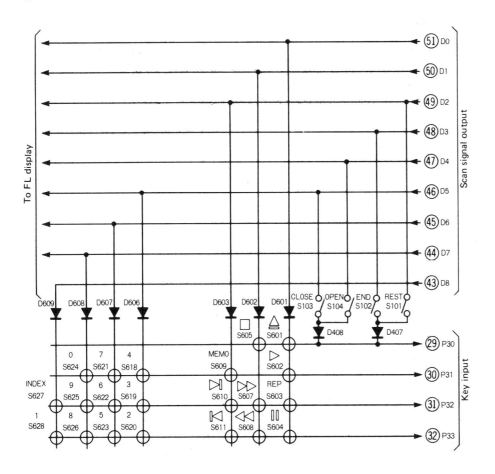

Fig. 9-2. Basic key matrix. *(Courtesy Technics)*

REMOTE-CONTROL SYSTEM

This model also has a wireless remote control. Interestingly enough, this system simply parallels the operation of the push buttons. The matrixing, however, is done internal to the remote-control decoder microprocessor, IC601. Fig. 9-3 shows how IC601 fits into the overall key matrix circuit. IC601 has nine inputs, corresponding to the output lines of IC401. These nine lines matrix to four output lines internal to IC601. When play is pressed on the remote-control unit, it will send out a modulated infrared beam to be received by the receiver circuit consisting of D800, the photodetector diode, and IC800, the remote signal amplifier and associated components. Fig. 9-4 shows that the signal from D800 enters IC800 at pin 1, then exits at pin 7 to drive the tuned amplifier/detector made of Q800 and T800. The detected signal is then amplified by IC800 once again before being sent to pin 26 of IC601. IC601 will decode the data and, according to which button on the remote was pressed, will connect the appropriate scan line to be appropriate output line.

Generation of the wireless code is done in the remote-control unit by IC1. Fig. 9-5 shows IC1 and a simplified key matrix which is used for its own push buttons. The scanning pulses are six lines wide, appearing at pins 8 through 13 of IC1. The input lines are seven lines wide, going into pins 14 through 21 of the IC. IC1 produces a different pattern of pulses for each of the 22 buttons (or functions) on the remote-control unit. These pulse patterns drive Q1, which in turn drives the infrared LED, D1. IC1, like all other microprocessors, is clock driven, and this is accomplished by crystal X1, connected between pins 4 and 5.

FRONT-PANEL DISPLAY

Another function of IC401 is the operation of the front-panel display. Twenty-two output lines from IC401 are used to drive the display (Fig. 9-3), which not surprisingly requires 22 control lines (plus one power line). The data for the display comes from the Q subcode channel which is delivered to IC401 pin 20, and comes from the LSI module, pin 14. There are about 76 individual elements of the display which must be illuminated to form the eight different 7-segment digits, and the track play indicator, as well as the special feature indicators. The 22 control lines from IC401 can control the 76 segments certainly not by a one-to-one drive, but by scanning them. Scanning means that not all of the display segments are lit at the same time, and this is the case. The 8 digits are scanned according to the digit itself and to which of the seven segments is to be lit. This creates a strobing effect that can actually be seen if one simply glances at the display. This method of driving a front-panel display is quite common, and is found in consumer tape decks, VCRs, and the like. The two LEDs inside the play button and pause button are illuminated from the control of IC401. A pause high signal at IC401 pin 39 and a play high signal at IC401 pin 40 drive Q406 and Q405, respectively. These two transistors drive the LEDs.

LOADING MOTOR CONTROL

Another function of IC401 is that of driving the loading motor to open and close the disc tray. The front-panel open/close switch, S601, must be pressed to open or close the door. If the door is open and a disc is placed in the tray, however, a light push on the door itself will initiate the closing operation. This occurs because the open position sensor, switch S104, opens when the tray is moved slightly by pushing. The door-open command appears at pin 37 of IC401, and the close command appears at pin 38. Refer to Fig. 9-6 to see the simplified block diagram of the door control circuit. Fig. 9-7 shows a partial schematic of the circuit. For the open command, pin 37 goes high and this is applied to pins 4 and 5 of IC653, and through the delay of R661, R662, and C654, to pin 3. A delayed low signal appears at pin 6, and is applied to pin 5 of IC402, the

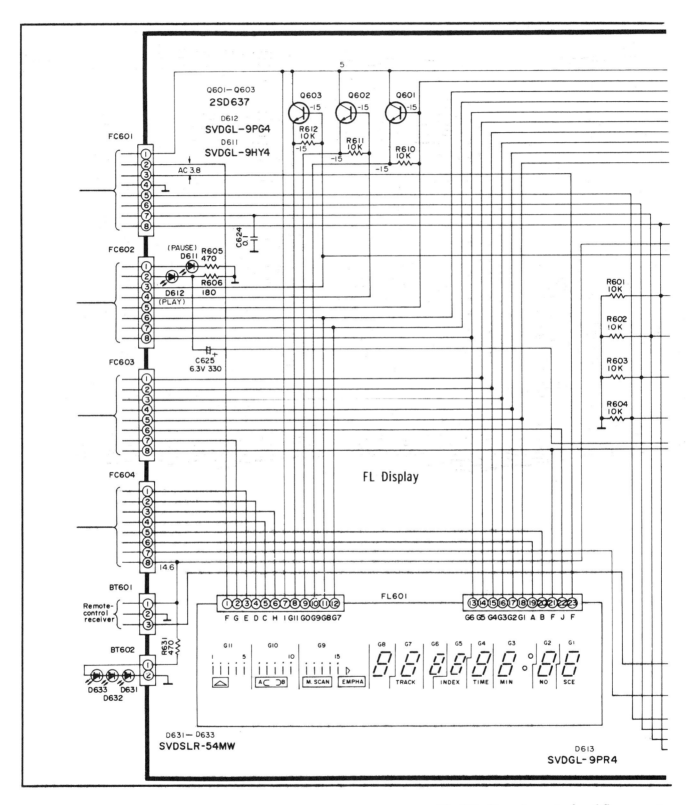

Fig. 9-3. Remote-control and fluorescent

loading motor control IC. At this, IC402 provides a high at pin 2 and a low at pin 10. The loading motor rotates in the open direction until the door-

open switch, S104, closes. When S104 closes, it signals IC401 to discontinue the open command. For the closing operation, pin 38 of IC401 goes

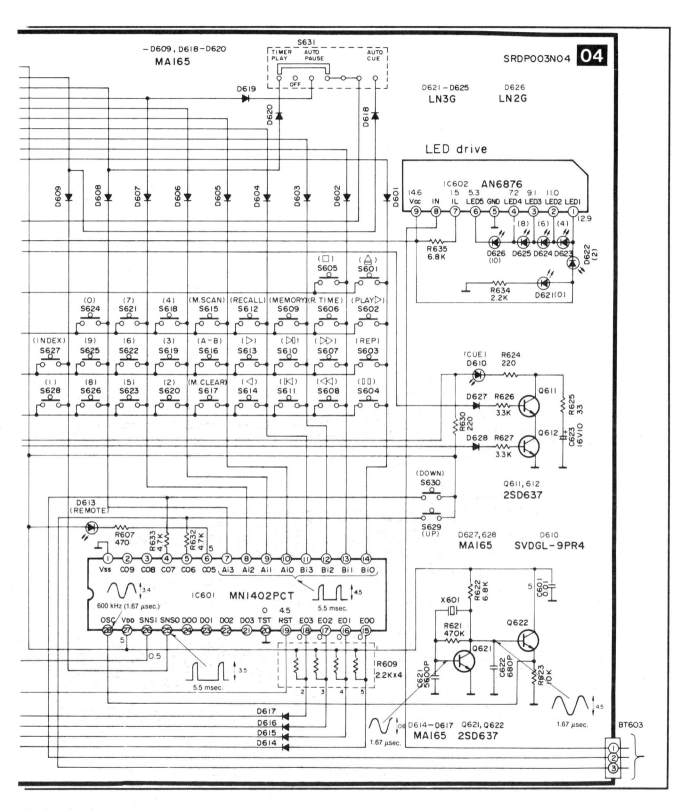

display circuits. *(Courtesy Technics)*

high and, in a similar way as was described for the open mode, a delayed low is produced by IC653, only at pin 10. This low is applied to IC402, pin 6. This causes pin 10 to go high, and pin 2 to go low, driving the loading motor in the reverse direction, closing the door. When the door closes fully, the door-close switch, S103, signals IC401 to drop the close command. At this point the unit will try to read the TOC, even if the play push button wasn't pressed.

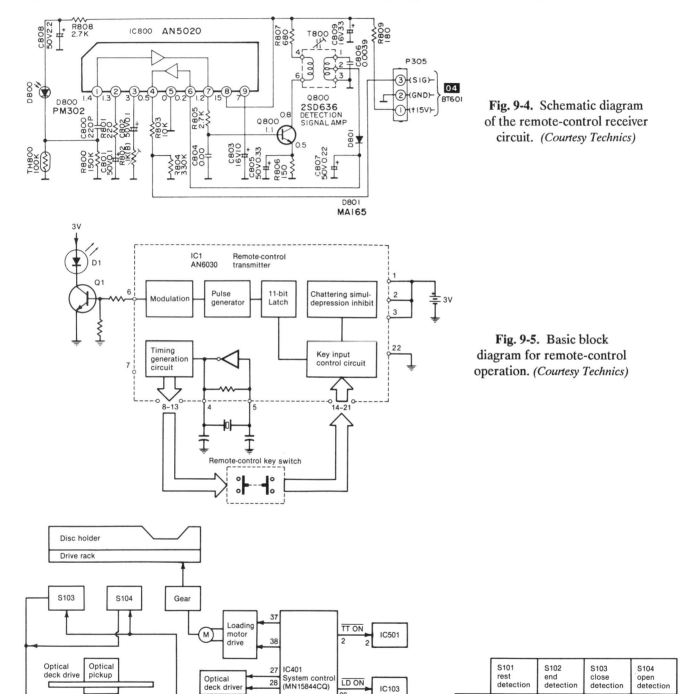

Fig. 9-4. Schematic diagram of the remote-control receiver circuit. *(Courtesy Technics)*

Fig. 9-5. Basic block diagram for remote-control operation. *(Courtesy Technics)*

(A) Simplified block diagram.

(B) On/off state of detection switch.

	S101 rest detection	S102 end detection	S103 close detection	S104 open detection
Open	On	Off	Off	On
Close	On	Off	On	Off
Play	Off	Off	On	Off

Fig. 9-6. Door control circuit. *(Courtesy Technics)*

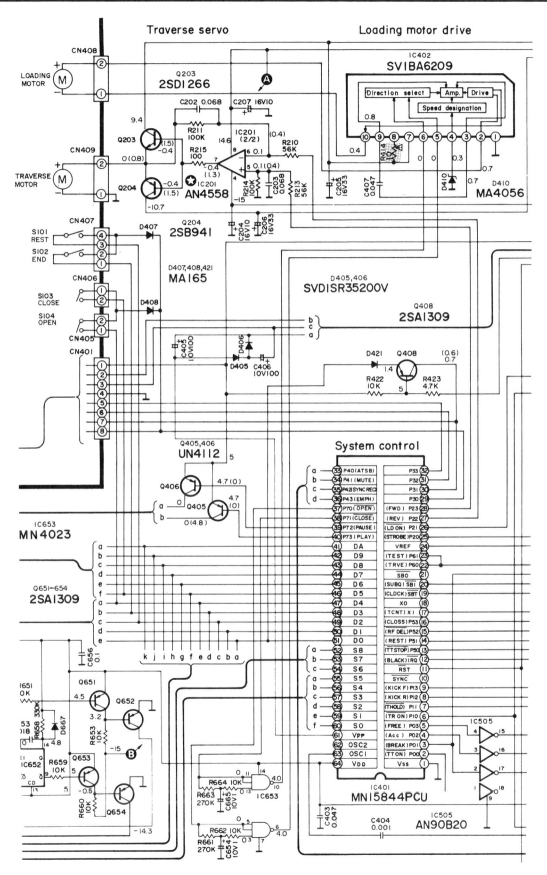

Fig. 9-7. Partial schematic showing IC401 and IC402 for loading motor control. *(Courtesy Technics)*

10

Before Making Adjustments

The compact audio disc player and the compact disc itself are high-technology products. More accurately, they are a perfect combination of high technologies, employing a laser, sophisticated error-correction techniques, and microprocessor control. Although no technician or hobbyist should ever be intimidated by such technology, it does require some amount of study before one acquires a sense of familiarity. Also, some degree of respect should be exercised when handling both the disc and the disc player.

HANDLING THE DISC

The compact disc has been highly touted as being nearly indestructible. Its durable plastic base, protected reflective layer, immunity to wear, and the error-correction capabilities of the player make it the dream medium. It may very well be the dream medium, but it is susceptible to damage from mishandling as any other medium is. First, consider the polycarbonate base. It is 1.2 millimeters thick and acts as the final optical element in the laser path. Polycarbonate is the material used for the interior windows in aircraft,

certainly proving its durability. But, as with all plastics, it is not scratchproof. If the disc is dropped, slid across a table, or stored carelessly, it will invariably become scratched. Now, due to the error-correction capabilities of the system, the effect of the majority of minor and moderate scratches can be compensated, and the disc will perform flawlessly. This is certainly no excuse to become sloppy in the handling of the disc. Since error correction operates "live" every time a disc is played, it is possible for the same scratch to cause a problem at some times during playback, and to be problem-free at other times. So, it is to the user's benefit to handle the CD with special care at all times, to avoid putting fingerprints on its playing surface, and to always store it in its "jewel box" storage case that it was sold in.

If fingerprints do occur, and it is necessary to clean them off, be sure to use a very soft, lint-free, clean cloth. Applying light pressure, move the cloth from the center of the disc outward, and never in a circular pattern. This action avoids placing even more scratches on the disc. If too much pressure is applied, scratches could be made, and if a circular motion is used, long circular scratches could be made. The latter may cause difficulty for the error-correction circuits, since a long stream of data may be missing, because the circular scratch could cover the circular tracks. Moving the cloth from the center to the outside will produce (if too much pressure is applied) short-term scratches, as they will be perpendicular to the disc's tracks.

The lacquer coating which protects the reflective, metallic coating is also a part of the disc which must be handled carefully. If something strikes the label side, it would only have to penetrate the thin lacquer coating to get to the reflective coating. If this happens, some of the reflective coating may be removed, and once this happens, the disc is permanently damaged. Although it is not advocated that technicians or hobbyists should go around intentionally damaging discs, the preceding cautions about handling the disc can be verified. If a known damaged disc is available, it is easy to see just how vulnerable the playing side is to scratches, and how vulnerable the reflective coating (under the label) is, by applying a small screwdriver lightly to the disc. Compact discs represent a sound investment (pun intended) and should be treated as such.

HANDLING THE PLAYER

The player is also subject to damage by mistreatment, primarily the optical assembly. Like a conventional turntable, the CD player is prone to shock or bumps while it is playing. Beyond this, everyday common sense applies. For example, dropping the unit can destroy the optical assembly. If anyone plays with the lens (if it is accessible) in the unit, its delicate suspension can be damaged. And in a troubleshooting situation, the optical assembly should never be forced into a particular position, or operated upside down. Again, these are common sense approaches to handling.

Before attempting to do work on the individual circuits inside the player, it is best to keep in mind the basic precautions necessary to handle MOS IC devices. Metallic-oxide semiconductor (MOS) devices are found in

virtually all brands and models of CD players, especially the system control ICs and other microprocessors, error-correction ICs, CIRC circuitry, and so on. The primary concern when dealing with MOS devices is that of damage through electrostatic discharge (ESD). When a unit is to be taken apart and the circuit boards handled, measures to ensure that the technician is not a carrier of an electrostatic charge should be taken. A technician can develop a static charge simply by shifting in the chair, or stepping over to the end of the bench to get a tool. The most common form of grounding for the technician is the wrist or ankle strap. The wrist strap is very much like a watch band, with a wire connecting it to a known ground through a resistance (typically 1 megohm or less). The ankle strap is similar. The technician is free to move, sit, stand, etc., without any concern for building up a static charge. Now, since the technician is grounded, extra care should be taken about getting electrical shocks. Even though there is a ground path resistor, there is no doubt that the ground path exists. Care should be exercised if it is necessary to operate the unit while the wrist strap is being worn.

SOLDERING AND DESOLDERING INTEGRATED CIRCUITS

While the unit is powered up, the technician is free to perform checks on the unit using test equipment, such as voltmeters and oscilloscopes. If a MOS IC is determined to be defective and should be replaced, the technician should use the same care he or she uses with all other MOS devices. Desoldering the defective component is of course necessary in order to remove it. It is important to use a grounded-tip soldering iron to perform this job, as certainly the technician wouldn't want to touch the hot tip in order to discharge any static buildup. And, by all means, since the soldering iron is grounded, the unit should be *turned off, with the ac plug disconnected.* This will prevent damage to the circuit in the event that a high-level signal or power line were to be grounded by the soldering iron.

The main trick in desoldering the device at this point will be dealing with the small pin size and the number of pins. The system control IC401, for example, has 64 pins. There are 64 individual soldering/desoldering jobs to perform here.

There are two basic types of multipin devices: surface-mounted components and through-mounted (through the board) components. Let's concentrate now on the newer, surface-mounted devices. The first task in removing such a device is to remove the solder at each pin. Removing as much solder as possible will make lifting each individual pin much easier. Removing solder is easily done with the use of a desoldering vacuum tool (solder sucker) or by using solder wick. Solder removal by vacuum requires heating each pin until the excess solder melts. Then, the prepared vacuum tool is placed next to the pin. The soldering iron is then removed and the vacuum tool is applied to the pin and activated. The liquid solder will be drawn into the reservoir of the tool. The bulb is then squeezed, ready to perform its vacuum action again. This procedure is repeated for each pin. Solder wick is a wire braid that makes use of the capillary action of melted solder. The many wires which make up the braid provide a large surface area on which the capillary action will take place. Solder wick is used while both it and the pin or pins are heated at the same time. This is done by placing the edge of the braid next to the tip of the iron. When the solder melts, and the braid is hot enough, the solder will be drawn into the braid, off of the pin or pins.

The excess solder from each pin must be removed before one tries to lift the pins away from the pc board. Once this is done, each individual pin will be lifted from the foil on the board. Raising the pins is done by heating one pin at a time until the solder which remains melts and the pin is free to be gently bent upward and off its foil pad. It is important that the solder be melted first before one gently pries up on the pin. If it is not, the foil pad itself may separate from the board and lift up with the pin. This is a serious condition, as the foil pad and the trace

that it is connected to are very delicate and can easily break off. Then, extra repairs would be necessary. The process of heating each pin and gently prying it off the foil pad must be done for each pin. The average pencil-tip soldering iron cannot be used to pry the pins up, but an assortment of soldering tools is widely available for this purpose. When all the pins are free, remove the IC. Before one begins to install the new IC the foil pads should be cleaned, to remove any dirt and old flux. Cleaning the pads makes installation (and future removal) of the new IC easier, and actually helps achieve a better solder connection.

Of course, a suspected defective IC wouldn't be removed unless a replacement IC was waiting by the side. This new IC will most likely be sold mounted in conductive foam or wrapped in metallic foil. This is how MOS ICs are shipped, stored, and sold, and it is done to prevent damage from static discharge. Such protective wrapping should not be removed until it is time to install the new IC, and not until the technician is grounded. Conceivably, a brand new IC can be ruined after it is unwrapped due to careless treatment by the technician. When all precautions have been taken, carefully remove the new IC from its foam, or unwrap it from the foil. Reckless treatment here could bend or break some pins. Place the new IC over the foil pads *in the same orientation* as was noted for the original IC. Heat each pin, one at a time, holding it over its proper pad, and apply a small amount of solder. When the solder melts, be sure the IC is positioned properly, and remove the iron. Then you should repeat this procedure for each of the pins.

For through-mounted ICs, those which have pins that are soldered on the far side (or bottom side) of the board onto which they're mounted, many of the same procedures apply. Perhaps the greatest difference is that individual pins cannot be pried up. The key to the removal of through-mounted components is to perform a good job of removing the excess solder from the pads on the foil side. As each pin is heated, the vacuum tool or solder wick is used to absorb the excess solder. All work is done, of course, from the foil side of the board. While the pad is still hot, try to center the pin in the hole, by bending it gently with the tip of the iron. Once the pin remains in the center of the hole on its own (without being held), remove the iron. That pin is now free for removal. This procedure must be repeated for each of the pins. If this job is performed properly, the IC will just fall out when the last pin is heated. Installing a new through-mounted component is also made easier if the pads are all cleaned first. Installing an IC like IC401 with 64 pins would require that all 64 pins be perfectly in line so that the IC drops right into the holes on the pc board. If the pins don't fit readily, they may be bent slightly, 32 at a time (one side at a time) by pressing the side of the IC into the grounded-mat work surface of the bench. Care should be taken not to overbend the pins. When the new IC fits into the holes *be sure it is oriented properly* and begin to solder each individual pin to its foil pad.

With luck, a component replacement will result in the total repair of the unit. If not, then more troubleshooting is required. Basic troubleshooting skills and practices are all that are necessary to investigate the various circuits. When you are troubleshooting MOS devices, some basic, common knowledge practices should be followed. The importance of a grounded work station (bench and mat) and resistance-grounded technician has already been covered. The use of high-input-impedance test equipment is recommended. If a test instrument has a really low input impedance, it could load down the high-impedance operation characteristic of MOS devices. Most modern voltmeters and oscilloscopes are of high input impedance. Also, as should be practiced in every case, be sure not to slip off of any pins when measuring, or to short two pins together. Grounding a power line or applying power to an undeserving pin has been known to destroy many an otherwise good IC.

11

Adjustments

Before working on any brand or model of a CD player, a technician should obtain the manufacturer's servicing literature. Only in this way can a technician have the reference material needed to perform the necessary troubleshooting procedures and repairs. Also, many manufacturers' service divisions maintain an update program, consisting of service bulletins and historical reports on a particular model. Subscribing to such services is also a good idea. A problem that makes some technicians pull out their hair could very well have been solved by someone else, and published in the service update literature. In a similar fashion, bona fide safety problems with a particular brand or model must be reported to authorized servicers or even to the public.

It is certainly impractical to cover the recommended adjustment procedures of all models of CD players from all manufacturers. But in order to cover some typical adjustments, and to be consistent, the adjustment procedures for the Technics SL-P2 will be covered. As is often the case, specific adjustment procedures from a manufacturer mimic the procedures performed at the factory, where the units are assembled. Sometimes special tools and test fixtures are required in order to produce specific

signals needed during the adjustments. The adjustment procedures for the SL-P2 require special test fixtures. As would be expected, one of these is a test disc complete with built-in dropouts. This test disc has the Technics part number SZZP1014F (Fig. 11-1). There are performance discs available but they will not work here, so be sure the proper test disc is on hand.

Another Technics test fixture is one called the traverse unit base (Fig. 11-2). This device is simply a holding stand for the entire optical assembly since it is necessary to have access to the test points and adjustments located on pc board 3, which is mounted on the optical assembly frame. These points and adjustments would otherwise be inaccessible because of the rather tight positioning of the optical assembly inside the player. In other words, the entire optical assembly in its frame (the traverse unit) will be physically removed from the chassis frame and mounted outside the unit on its stand. One very important point to remember here is that one should *never look into lens* when the unit is powered *on*. In fact, just make it a general practice never to put one's face over the lens assembly. The laser is not very strong, but it *is* a laser and could be capable of injuring the eye.

Fig. 11-1. Test disc. *(Courtesy Technics)*

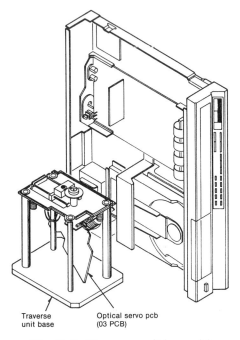

Traverse   Optical servo pcb
unit base   (03 PCB)

Fig. 11-2. Traverse unit base with
SL-P2. *(Courtesy Technics)*

Another test fixture is the servo gain adjuster, with Technics part number SZZP1017F (Fig. 11-3). This is actually a small piece of test equipment designed especially for SL-P2 (and other SL-P models). A third test fixture is an adaptor cable, called a "conversion connector" (Fig. 11-4). The servo gain adjuster can be used on other SL-P models, but the conversion

connector will supply only those signals necessary for the alignment of the SL-P2.

Assume at this point that it is known that the entire optical assembly (traverse unit) will have to be removed for adjustment, and that special test fixtures are needed in order to perform the adjustments. But why go through all of this in the first place? Although it is possible for the optical circuits simply to be in need of adjustment, it is more likely that it will be necessary to replace the optical block because of a worn or otherwise defective laser, and/or focus/tracking coil assembly.

All CD player service manuals contain information pertaining to the removal of the optical block, or laser and lens assembly. For the Technics SL-P2 the traverse unit must first be removed according to the complete removal procedures found in the service literature, and then the laser optical assembly can be removed. When it is replaced, the adjustments controlling the operation of the electro-optical circuits must be performed—as in the factory when an optical/lens assembly is mated with a traverse unit.

Once a new optical assembly has been installed into the traverse unit, the traverse unit must be mounted onto the traverse base fixture. Once in this position, the traverse unit will be able to spin and play a disc even while it is outside the player—provided that the disc is held in place on the spindle with the disc clamp magnet. The magnet must be removed from its normal mount in the door assembly for this purpose. Of course it is presumed that the unit had been disassembled at some time previously. In order to perform the various adjustments, the front panel must be reinstalled (partially). The test equipment which must be on hand includes:

1. Two-channel, external trigger oscilloscope (30-megahertz bandwidth or greater).

2. Digital voltmeter.

3. Audio-frequency oscillator.

Then, in order to do the adjustments, connect the 13-pin plug of the conversion connector to the 13-pin socket (the extended wire connector) of the servo gain adjuster. The 13-pin socket connector of the conversion adaptor must then be con-

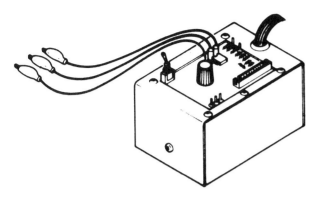

Fig. 11-3. Servo gain adjuster. *(Courtesy Technics)*

nected to the board mounted 13-pin plug on the adjuster. Connectors CN405, CN406, and CN408 from the traverse unit should then be reconnected to their proper connectors in the traverse unit. If the traverse unit is mounted to the base fixture, do it now (but the optical servo board must be removed first). Then reconnect CN407, CN409, CN411 and CN501 to the main unit. Next, remove the shorting pin jack connected to CN103 on the main unit's optical servo board, and connect the 5-pin socket connector from the conversion connector in its place. Everything is set now for the first adjustment.

FOCUS GAIN ADJUSTMENT

With the servo gain adjuster connected as previously described, connect its three alligator clip leads as follows:

Red ... to +15 volts (wire jumper off of pin 13 of IC301).
Blue ... to −15 volts (wire jumper off of pin 12 of IC301).
Green ... to chassis ground (see Fig. 11-5).

Now, do the following:

1. Adjust the audio-frequency oscillator to 750 hertz, at a level of 150 millivolts peak to peak. Connect this signal to the TEST OSC input connectors on the gain adjuster (observe polarity).

2. Connect the oscilloscope:
   Channel 1 to the gain adjuster's TP1.
   Channel 2 to the gain adjuster's TP2.
   TP3 is ground.

3. Set the oscilloscope:
   100 millivolts per division (both channels).
   Sweep to 2 milliseconds per division.
   AC coupling.
   CHOP mode.

4. Turn the switch on the gain adjuster to position 1.

5. Place the test disc on the spindle, with clamping magnet.

6. Turn the player's power on. When the disc starts, two traces of a 750-hertz sine wave will appear on the scope.

7. Adjust VR101 so that the amplitudes of both TP1 and TP2 waveforms are equal (see Fig. 11-6).

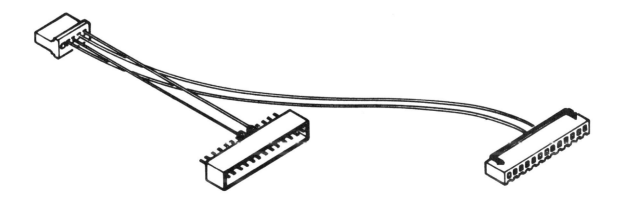

Fig. 11-4. Conversion connector. *(Courtesy Technics)*

FOCUS BALANCE CONTROL ADJUSTMENT

1. Remove the oscillator signal from the gain adjuster, which was used for the previous adjustment. Set the selector switch to position 2, and turn the power switch on.

2. Using a clip lead, connect test point TJ102 on the optical servo board to ground.

3. Remove the jumper plug from connector CN501 on the optical servo board.

4. Connect the oscilloscope:

   Channel 1 to test point TJ101 on the optical servo board.

5. Set the oscilloscope:

   Channel 1 to 500 millivolts per division.
   Sweep to 5 milliseconds per division.
   AC coupling.

6. Place the test disc on the spindle and secure it with the magnetic clamp.

7. Turn the player on. The focus-error S-curve will appear on the scope. Adjust VR102 so that the peaks on the S-curve are symmetrical, as shown in Fig. 11-7.

Since this adjustment interrupts the normal focusing action, the TOC will not be read, and the unit will stop after about 5 seconds. This is a mighty short time in which to make an adjustment. To keep the laser on approximately 2 minutes, use a clip lead and ground pin 4 of connector CN412 on the main board, after the laser has already gone on. (There is only about 5 seconds in which to do this.)

When you are finished, remove the clip leads from CN412, and TJ102. Also, reconnect the jumper to CN501.

FOCUS OFFSET ADJUSTMENT

1. Leave the gain adjuster as it was for the previous adjustment (power switch on, and rotary switch to number 2).

2. Press the open/close switch so that the door opens.

3. Connect the digital voltmeter to test point TJ101 on the optical servo board.

4. Adjust VR103 so that the voltage is 0 volts with a tolerance of ± 10 millivolts.

TRACKING GAIN ADJUSTMENT

1. Leave the power switch of the gain adjuster on, but set the rotary switch to position 3.

2. Set the audio-frequency oscillator:

   1.5-kilohertz frequency.
   150-millivolt peak-to-peak output.

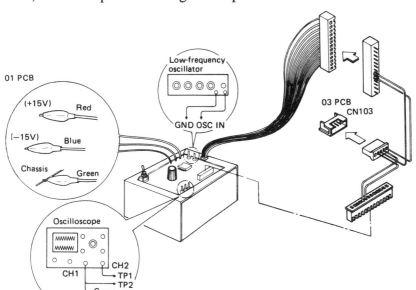

Fig. 11-5. Connection of the servo gain adjuster.
(Courtesy Technics)

3. Connect the oscilloscope:

Channel 1 to TP1 of the gain adjuster.
Channel 2 to TP2 of the gain adjuster.
TP3 is ground.

4. Set the oscilloscope:

100 millivolts per division, both channels.
Sweep 2 milliseconds.
AC coupling.
CHOP mode.

5. Be sure the test disc and magnetic clamp are in place on the spindle.

6. Turn the player on. When the disc spins, a 1.5-kilohertz signal will appear on both traces of the scope. Adjust VR104 so that the amplitudes of both channels are the same (see Fig. 11-8).

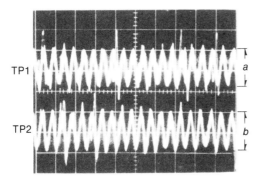

Fig. 11-6. Focus gain adjustment TP1 and TP2 amplitudes are equal. *(Courtesy Technics)*

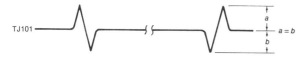

Fig. 11-7. Focus balance adjustment positive-peak and negative-peak amplitudes are equal. *(Courtesy Technics)*

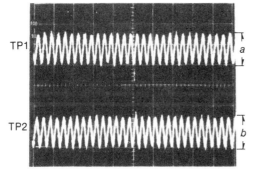

Fig. 11-8. Tracking gain adjustment TP1 and TP2 amplitudes are equal. *(Courtesy Technics)*

TRACKING OFFSET COARSE ADJUSTMENT

1. Leave the power switch of the gain adjuster on, but set the selector switch to position 2. Remove the oscillator signal that was used in the previous adjustment.

2. Press the door open/close switch so that the door opens.

3. Connect the digital voltmeter to test point TJ103 on the optical servo board.

4. Adjust VR106 so that the voltage reads 0 volts with a tolerance of ±3 millivolts.

TRACKING BALANCE ADJUSTMENT

1. Be sure that the power switch of the gain adjuster is on, and that the rotary selector is set to position 2.

2. Connect the oscilloscope:

Channel 1 to test point TJ103 on the optical servo board.

3. Set the oscilloscope:

Channel 1 to 200 millivolts per division.
Sweep to 5 milliseconds per division.
DC coupling.

4. Put the test disc and magnetic clamper on the spindle.

5. Turn the player on. Allow several seconds for the disc to come up to speed, then turn the tracking error (TE) switch on the gain adjuster to its off position.

6. The tracking error signal will appear on the scope. Adjust VR105 so that the waveform is symmetrical about the zero axis, as shown in Fig. 11-9.

TRACKING OFFSET FINE ADJUSTMENT

1. Leave the gain adjuster set the way it was for the previous adjustment (power on, select position 2).

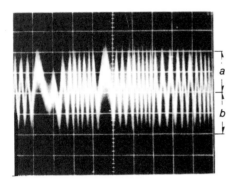

Fig. 11-9. Tracking balance adjustment: adjust for zero-axis symmetry—when positive and negative peaks are equal in amplitude. *(Courtesy Technics)*

2. Press the door open/close switch so that the door opens.

3. Connect the digital voltmeter to test point TJ103 on the optical servo board.

4. Adjust VR106 so that the voltmeter reads 0 volts with a tolerance of ±3 millivolts.

After completing these adjustments, remove the servo gain adjuster and reconnect the jumper plug to connector CN103.

OFFSET ADJUSTMENT DURING DROPOUT

1. Connect the oscilloscope:

   Channel 1 to test point TJ101 on the optical servo board.

   Channel 2 to test point TJ103, on the same board.

   EXT trigger to test point TJ104 on the main board.

2. Set the oscilloscope:

   1 volt per division for both channels.
   Sweep to 0.5 millisecond.
   AC coupling.
   Trigger to EXT NORMAL.

3. Place the test disc and clamper on the spindle. Play back track 13. This is the dropout test.

4. Two dropout waveforms will appear on the scope. While watching the channel 1 trace, adjust VR103 so that the dropout pulse is minimized. (This pulse may not be readily visible unless VR103 is intentionally misadjusted.)

5. Watch the channel 2 trace on the scope, and adjust VR106 so that the dropout pulse is minimized, following the same procedure in step 4. See Fig. 11-10.

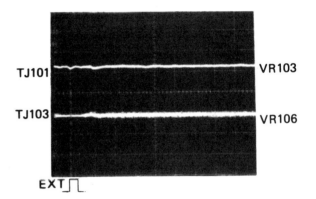

Fig. 11-10. Dropout offset adjustment. The dropout pulse for both channels should be minimized. *(Courtesy Technics)*

BEST EYE ADJUSTMENT

The "eye" adjustment is a term that simply refers to the amplitude of the RF signal. A string of sine waves is what the RF signal looks like on the scope, and the area between the top and bottom peaks is called the "eye pattern."

1. Connect the oscilloscope:

   Channel 1 to test point TJ402 on the main board.

2. Set the oscilloscope:

   Channel 1 to 1 volt per division.
   Sweep to 0.5 microsecond per division.
   AC coupling.

3. Play the test disc at track number 1.

4. The RF signal will appear on the scope. Adjust VR102 so that its amplitude becomes maximum (see Fig. 11-11).

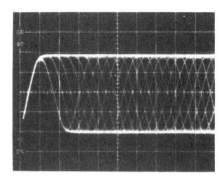

Fig. 11-11. Best eye adjustment. Adjust VR102 so that the amplitude of the waveform is maximum. *(Courtesy Technics)*

PHASE-LOCKED LOOP ADJUSTMENT

1. Press the door switch so that the door opens.
2. Connect the oscilloscope:

   Channel 1 to test point TJ701 (FCLK) on the main board.
   Channel 2 to test point TJ702 (CLDCK) on the same board.

3. Set the oscilloscope:

   2 volts per division for both channels.
   Sweep to 20 microseconds per division.
   AC coupling.
   Trigger to NORMAL, Negative Slope.
   ALTernate mode.

4. Use a clip lead and connect pin 13 of IC301 on the main board to ground.
5. The scope will show the FCLK (channel 1) and CLDCK (channel 2) signals. Adjust coil L301 so that both pulses line up as shown in Fig. 11-12.
6. Now remove the clip lead that was used in step 4.
7. Turn VR501 fully clockwise.
8. Play back the test disc at track 1.
9. When the playback has started, use a clip lead to connect test point TJ501 on the main board to ground.

10. Again view the two waveforms, and adjust VR501 so that the *falling* edges of both pulses are coincident, as shown in Fig. 11-13.

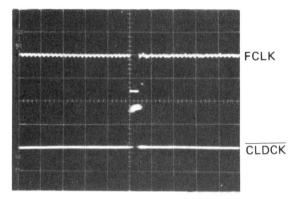

Fig. 11-12. PLL adjustment. Adjust coil L301 so that the pulses are centered with respect to each other. *(Courtesy Technics)*

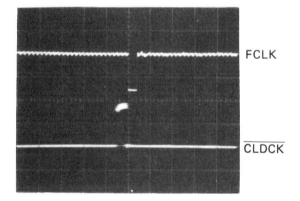

Fig. 11-13. PLL adjustment. Adjust VR501 so that the pulses line up as shown.
(Courtesy Technics)

On completion of these adjustments all functions of the unit should be checked. That is, be sure that playback is normal and that the skip and search functions work well. Additionally, play back the test disc at track 12. This track contains black spots on the polycarbonate surface to simulate scratches. The disc should play back with no noise or dropouts. Also, play back track 14. This is the track that simulates fingerprints, as it contains permanent smudge marks on the surface of the polycarbonate. It, too, should play back without any noise or dropout. Both of these test bands contain warble tones, so that there is some signal from which to identify performance problems. If there are any problems with playback, either the adjustments were performed poorly, or incompletely, or the traverse unit or optical assembly is defective.

Fig. 11-14 shows a troubleshooting diagram to use if the traverse unit and optical assembly are suspected of being defective. It follows the path of the adjustments that were performed, so that in such a case when the optics are suspected, it recommends repeating some of the adjustments.

Beyond this, it also suggests a few mechanical adjustments that must be checked. Generally, the mechanical adjustments will not very often drift from the factory settings, but in cases of abuse, tampering, etc., it may be necessary to check them. As might be guessed, three test fixtures are required. They are the rest position gauge (part number SZZP1019F), feeler gauge (part number SZZP1020F), and the grating adjustment tool (part number SZZP1018F). These are shown in

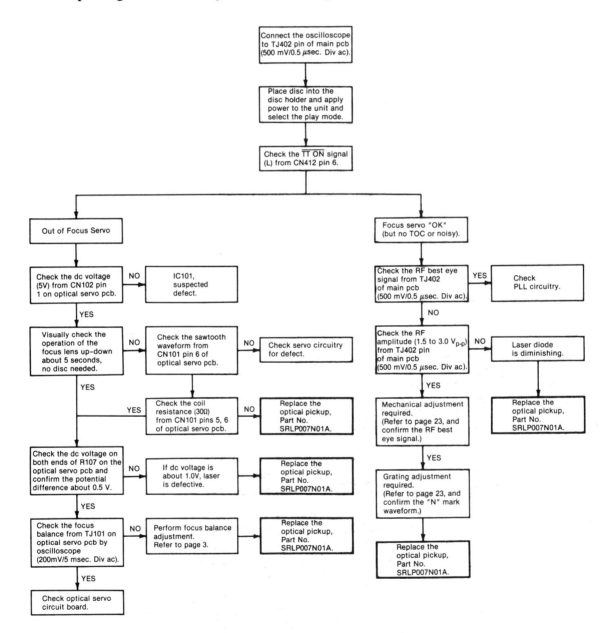

Fig. 11-14. Adjustment procedure flowchart. *(Courtesy Technics)*

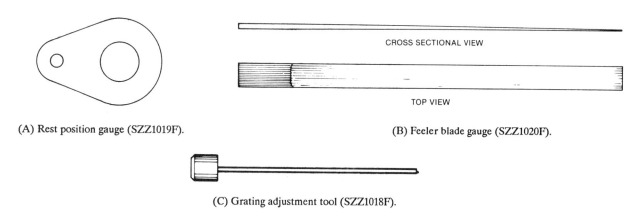

(A) Rest position gauge (SZZ1019F). (B) Feeler blade gauge (SZZ1020F).

(C) Grating adjustment tool (SZZ1018F).

Fig. 11-15. Mechanical adjustment fixtures. *(Courtesy Technics)*

Fig. 11-15. Also required are the 30 MHz two-channel oscilloscope, test disc, regular disc, hex wrench kit, and gauge kit (part number SZZP1022F).

REST POSITION ADJUSTMENT

1. Be sure that the rest and end switches haven't been damaged during disassembly of the traverse unit. If they are bent, they can be bent carefully back to their normal shapes. (These are leaf type switches that should normally have a leaf space of about 2 millimeters.)
2. Turn the player on, which will cause the optics to move to the rest position.
3. Turn off the power to the player.
4. Place the rest position gauge over the turntable and lens as shown in the diagram in Fig. 11-16A.
5. The lens should rest in the center of the gauge's lens hole, as shown. If it is too near to, or too far from, the spindle, loosen the lock screw, and turn the rest position adjustment until the lens is centered. Refer to Figs. 11-16B through 11-16D.
6. Recheck by playing a disc, then stopping and removing the disc. Turn the power off and then on again to see if the rest position is proper.

TURNTABLE HEIGHT ADJUSTMENT*

1. Remove the jumper plug from connector CN103 on the optical servo board. This disables the focus search routine.
2. Insert the feeler gauge between the turntable and the shaft bearing as shown in Fig. 11-17A.
3. In this position, slide the feeler gauge through toward its thick end, and mark it with a pencil at the point where it becomes snug.
4. Connect the oscilloscope to test point TJ402 on the main board.
5. Turn the player on. Press the door-open button, then the door-close button.
6. Confirm that the RF signal appears on the scope. *If not, proceed to step 7.*
7. While playing, gently tap the moving disc at arrow A as shown in Fig. 11-17B. If the RF signal appears, the turntable is too low. If not, tap the disc at arrow B. If the RF signal appears, the turntable is too high.

Corrective Steps

(*a*) Insert the feeler gauge as was done before in step 3, at the point marked by the pencil.

---
* This is necessary if the spindle motor was replaced.

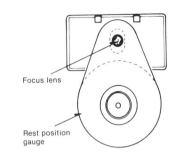

(A) Rest position gauge on turntable— proper adjustment.

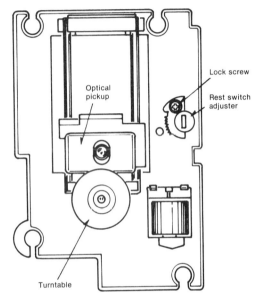

(B) Location of turntable, lock screw, and adjustment.

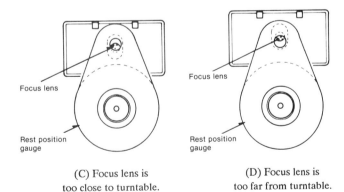

(C) Focus lens is too close to turntable.

(D) Focus lens is too far from turntable.

Fig. 11-16. Use of rest position gauge.
(Courtesy Technics)

(*b*) Loosen the hexagonal set screw as shown in Fig. 11-17A.

(*c*) If the turntable was too low, slide the gauge about $1/8$ inch (3.175 millimeters) towards its thick end to raise the height.

(*d*) If the turntable was too high, move the gauge about $1/8$ inch (3.175 millimeters) towards its thin end to lower the height.

(*e*) Again play the disc and check for the RF signal.

(*f*) If the signal is not present, then this "trial and error" method must be repeated.

Note: When you are finished, be sure to reconnect the jumper plug to connector CN103.

GRATING ADJUSTMENT

1. Place the test disc on the turntable with the magnetic clamper.

2. Connect the oscilloscope:

   Channel 1 to test point TJ402 on the main board.
   Channel 2 to pin 17 of IC104 of the optical servo board.

3. Set the oscilloscope:

   1 volt per division for both channels.
   Sweep to 2 microseconds per division.
   AC coupling.

4. Turn unit on and play the disc at track 1.

5. If the two waveforms appear on the scope as shown in Fig. 11-18, then the adjustment is good. *If not, go to step 6.*

6. Insert the grating adjustment tool in the optical block as shown in Fig. 11-18A.

7. Carefully turn the tool either clockwise or counterclockwise until the "N mark" in the channel 2 waveform appears, and the RF waveform in channel 1 is maximum (see Fig. 11-18B).

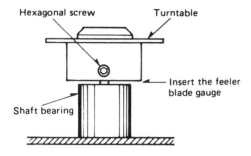

(A) Front view of traverse unit showing where feeler gauge should be inserted.

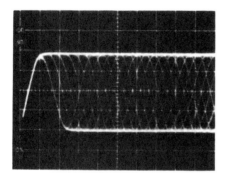

RF signal

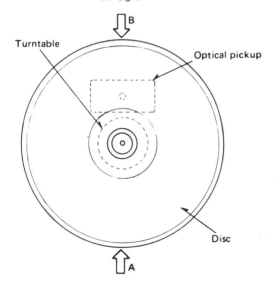

(B) Adjusting the height of the turntable.

Fig. 11-17. Turntable height adjustment.
(Courtesy Technics)

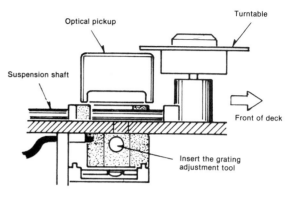

(A) Showing where grating adjustment tool should be inserted.

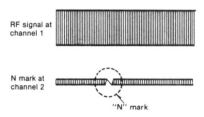

(B) Showing that channel 1 should be maximized while the "N" mark on channel 2 is present.

Fig. 11-18. The grating adjustment. *(Courtesy Technics)*

8. Carefully follow the manufacturer's procedures for reassembly.

12

Troubleshooting

In this chapter a practical and comprehensive approach to troubleshooting the SL-P2 will be discussed. Sometimes, however, the terms "practical" and "comprehensive" are relative. Certainly some reports are more practical and comprehensive than others. That is to say, no troubleshooting guide can be so complete as to guess and list every possible failure for a particular product, and then go on to state which repairs will fix the problem. But any good troubleshooting guide will be able to pinpoint the problem area and suggest the most likely cause or causes of a problem. No formula exists, however, which will tell a technician which component or part of the equipment should be changed based on a one-time description of the problem (short of a blown fuse!).

The technician should also be equipped with a minimum of test gear, namely, the test fixtures, the service manual or other literature, voltmeter, oscilloscope, hand tools, soldering/desoldering equipment, amplifier and speakers, grounding strap and grounded work station, master ac power switch for safety, and a complete report of the problem.

REPORTING THE PROBLEM

Just as a medical doctor will ask specific questions when a patient visits, the technician should get a clear report of the problem from the consumer. In many service shops, however, the technician is not the person who deals with the consumer; that is handled by the receptionist or counterperson. But whether or not the technician gets to speak personally with the consumer, a detailed list of the problem or problems must be written down. In most cases it is written on a service ticket or service form. Complaints such as "doesn't work right," or "it skips by itself," are insufficient and can waste the technician's time. If the two complaints above were refined to "the disc spins, but the display never appears," and "two of my CDs cause the unit to skip," the technician can go right to work *verifying* the problem, not *hunting* for it. Some consumers may get testy about answering questions about their unit that failed, but it should be explained in these cases that if a precise description of the problem is given, the unit will most likely get fixed sooner.

Nonverifiable problems rarely happen, but it still is a good idea for the technician or service manager to call the consumer at home to get a better description of the problem, or to state that the problem cannot be verified. Questions to ask the consumer over the phone or in person would be ones that determine the frequency of the problem, i.e., "Does this happen all the time and with every disc?" To find the general area of the problem, ask, "Did you notice if the disc is spinning?" or, "Is there any playback sound?" or, "Does the display change as the disc plays?" or "Is the table of contents displayed shortly after the disc is inserted?" There are many more variations of questions, depending on the initial report and on the consumer's answers. It certainly would help the technician to become familiar with the normal operation of the model in question. Even different but similar models will enlighten the technician as to what is normal operation. In this regard some customer problems are a matter of education, that is, the customers simply have not understood the operating instructions. In these cases the unit is not malfunctioning, and it is up to the technician to recognize this.

VERIFYING THE PROBLEM

Once the unit is in the hands of the technician, it is put on the bench and evaluated for performance. Specifically, the problem as described by the customer will be verified, if possible. Certainly, a blown main fuse will produce the symptom of "no playback sound," but the technician should also note that there will be no panel lights and no operation of the disc door, etc. It is now time for the technician to start using his or her eyes, ears, and nose. Things to look for include the smooth rotation of the spindle motor, the lighting of the display, or smoke. Listen for the normal chattering sound as the table of contents is read and the first selection is played. This sound emanates from the lens assembly as it is being driven by both the focus coil and tracking coils. (It actually does behave somewhat as the

voice coil of a speaker.) The sense of smell is a reliable way to detect overheating and smoke. Not only is using the senses important, it is usually accurate.

Of equal importance is that of not being intimidated by sophisticated products. In circuits where microprocessors are used, the microprocessors are often suspected as being the culprits simply because they are complex and not fully understood. Under no circumstances should the microprocessor be blamed simply on the grounds that it has so many jobs to do. History shows that it is the electromechanical devices which fail, at far more regular intervals than do microprocessors. Simple items like dc motors, switches, belts, mechanical linkage, fuses, poor solder joints, loose connectors, loose screws, pinched wires, broken traces on the pc boards, etc., are all more likely to be the cause of a malfunction than a microprocessor. Keep the microprocessor in its proper perspective. It has many pins, because it makes and receives many signals. We only have to be concerned with one circuit area at a time, and we can check the microprocessor for the signals it sends and takes from that circuit. Basically, computer chips are very reliable, so look for something mechanical, something prone to wear or stress or heat, look for a link or a motor to jam, or a belt to slip off or break, and check the microprocessor as the last resort.

REVIEWING THE BASICS

An overview of each of the main circuits will be given here, to serve as a review and quick reference. The overview states the major functions of each circuit and the most likely symptoms produced if a failure in this section occurs.

Optical Playback System

This is the three-beam (SL-P2) generation and detection system which uses a laser to create the beams and produce the playback RF data.

Major Functions

1. Read the pits/flats (recover data).
2. Generate a focus error voltage signal (and respond to the focus error drive signal).
3. Generate a tracking error signal (and respond to the tracking error drive signal).

Symptoms of Failure

1. Table of contents (TOC) not read.
2. No playback.

Focus Servo—The focus servo circuit operates on the focus error signal developed by the optics. It generates a focus error drive signal to correct an out-of-focus condition.

Symptoms of Failure

1. Table of contents (TOC) not read.
2. Unusually long time required to read TOC (about 10 seconds).
3. Unstable or an inconsistent reading of TOC (incorrect display).

Tracking Servo

This servo circuit operates on the tracking error signal developed by the optics, and it is used to keep the lens on track at all times. The tracking error drive signal is generated by this circuit and is used to drive the four tracking coils on the lens assembly.

Symptoms of Failure

1. The CD skips (track jumping).
2. TOC is not read.
3. Unit stays in the search mode.

Traverse Servo

This circuit operates on the tracking error drive

signal, and when the voltage exceeds a pre-determined level it will signal the system control IC to generate a traverse motor command, either forward or reverse. This forward or reverse command will energize a drive circuit to move the traverse motor.

Symptoms of Failure

1. Unit will not skip or search (will not perform track access).
2. TOC is not read.
3. Erratic operation of skip or search.

RF Data Pickup

This circuit takes the playback RF signal, and through the operation of a phase-locked loop will detect the EFM and PCK signals.

Symptoms of Failure

1. TOC is not read.
2. Erratic operation of the optics.
3. Playback noise (if the PLL loses lock).

Spindle Motor Servo

This circuit is responsible for starting the spindle motor and keeping the disc spinning at a constant linear velocity. It operates under control of the system control IC (the ACC signal) and from the playback EFM signal (11T). Fine control is achieved by comparing the playback frame clock to the crystal-controlled frame clock.

Symptoms of Failure

1. Disc docs not spin.
2. Abnormal spinning of the disc.
3. Skipping.
4. TOC is not read.

Loading Motor

Under control of the system control IC, this circuit opens and closes the disc tray (door).

Symptoms of Failure

1. Door will not open/close.
2. Disc rubs the lens assembly.

EFM Decoding/Error Correction

This circuit receives the playback EFM signal and decodes it into 16-bit digital audio samples and the subcode channels.

Symptoms of Failure

1. TOC is not read.
2. Gross playback noise.
3. No sound.

Audio Processing

This circuit converts the 16-bit digital audio into analog. Deserialization (deglitching) is performed as well as phase restoration of the left channel.

Symptoms of Failure

1. One or both channels not working.
2. Gross playback noise.

System Control

This is the main control for all of the unit's operations. It also calculates the display data, and drives the display. Key servo signals are generated ($\overline{\text{TR ON}}$, $\overline{\text{CLDCK}}$, $\overline{\text{TT ON}}$, etc.) Muting is controlled by this IC, as well as mechanism commands (KICK, OPEN, CLOSE, etc.)

Symptoms of Failure

1. No operation (but unit isn't dead).
2. TOC is not read.
3. Erratic system operation.

Remote Control

This device has self-contained circuitry for wireless code generation. The receiver is in the player, and parallels the operation of the front-panel push buttons.

Symptoms of Failure

1. Remote control doesn't work (new batteries).
2. Erratic operation of remote control.
3. Unit changes mode by itself.

VERIFYING THE POWER SUPPLY

Troubleshooting any electronic device must absolutely begin by confirming the proper operation of the power supply, and its various outputs. The power supply board for the SL-P2 is board number 6. It consists of regulators IC1, IC2, and IC3, along with regulator Q1. IC4 and IC5 are *fuses*. The following checklist is what's normal for the operation of the power supply. Refer to Fig. 12-1 while reading this list.

IC1, pin 3	+15 volts
IC2, pin 3	−15 volts
IC3, pin 3	+5 volts
IC4, pin 2	+10 volts
IC5, pin 2	−10 volts
Connector BT-2, measure across pins 5 and 6 for 3.6 V ac	
Connector BT-2, pin 7	−15 volts

If any of these voltages are missing, the unit will not operate correctly. This information will help, in the event of a problem, pinpoint the area on the power supply board.

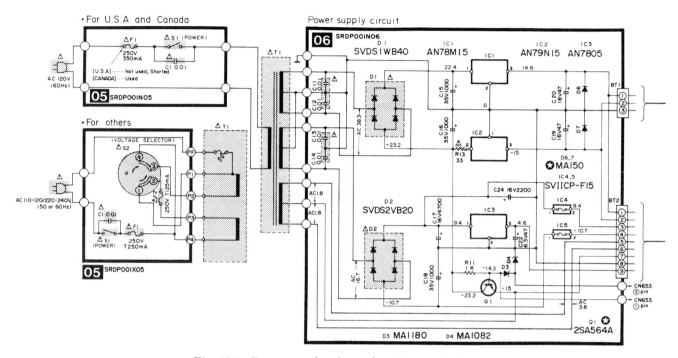

Fig. 12-1. Power supply schematic. *(Courtesy Technics)*

Power Distribution

The voltages listed above will appear throughout the unit. This section provides, at a glance, a knowledge of which power supply voltages should be seen at various ICs in the various circuits. This applies only to the SL-P2, but it is representative of what kind of information is available for most units that are worked on. If the information is not provided by the manufacturer, a list can still be made from a known good unit. Fig. 12-2 shows, in block form, where all the power supply voltages are sent.

VERIFYING THE LOADING MOTOR

We will start with the simplest circuit, the loading motor. Referring back to chapter 9, Fig. 9-6 contains a block diagram showing the door open/close switches and the optics rest and end switches. Included is a truth table showing the conditions of the switches. Notice that during play, both the rest and end detection switches are open, since the optics are neither at the TOC location (rest), nor at the outermost periphery of the disc (end). Failure of the disc tray to operate

would indicate either a failure of the loading motor drive IC or failure of the system control IC to generate an open or close command.

If the command is not being issued, the key matrix should be checked. Fig. 12-3 shows a simplified key matrix, and the open/close front-panel switch is S601. This switch will tie the scan output at IC401 pin 51 to pin 29. Checking with a scope at pin 51 should reveal a pulse train signal, if normal. Checking with a scope at pin 29 will reveal a waveform that will *change* when the open/close switch is pressed. If this action does take place and the IC still does not generate an open/close command, then IC401 is to be suspected. This method of checking the key matrix circuit to see that scanning pulses are being tied to the appropriate input can be used for all modes, if the particular mode can't be entered.

CHECKING THE OPERATION OF FOCUS SERVO

A simplified block diagram of the focus servo circuit and its associated components is shown in Fig. 12-4. No operation at all can be performed if

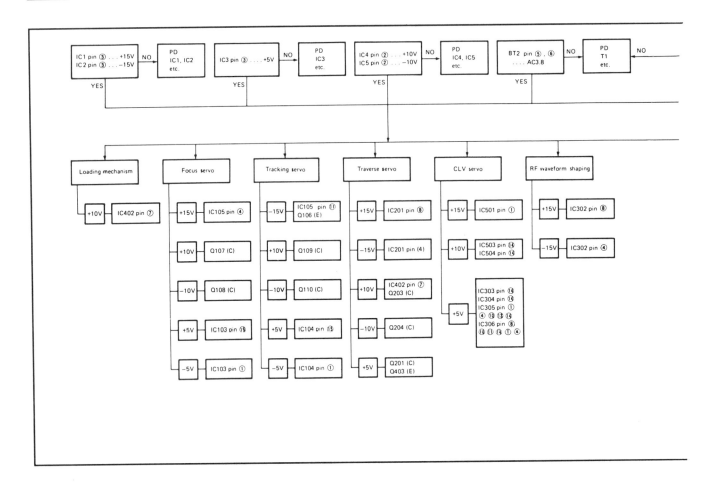

Fig. 12-2. Troubleshooting diagram for

the laser diode isn't activated. To confirm this, check pin 26 of IC401 to see if the $\overline{\text{LD ON}}$ active-low signal has indeed gone low. Next, the focus search operation can be checked by looking *perpendicularly* at the focus lens. This can only be done when the unit is apart. When the play button is pressed, the laser should be turned on and the focus lens will search for a range of focus. The lens can actually be seen to move up and down with a rather large excursion seven or eight times per second. If the focus lens does search, then it's time to play a disc and to check for the RF signal at test point TJ402. There should be an easily discernible sinusoidal pattern. Checking at test point TJ401, the $\overline{\text{RF DET}}$ active-low signal should be low. The $\overline{\text{RF DEL}}$ (RF delay) active-low signal at pin 15 of IC401 should be checked to see if it is low. And if it is, then a focus error signal should be available at pin 18 of IC103. If these items seem to be function-

ing alright, then there should be no problems with the focus circuit. If the items are not as stated, then more checking is necessary, and can be conducted according to the following figures. Fig. 12-5A indicates items that must be checked without a disc in place. It is really a recapitulation of the procedure just mentioned, but because it is in block form it can be more readily understood. Fig. 12-5B shows the checks that should be performed while playing a disc.

CHECKING THE OPERATION OF THE TRACKING SERVO

The simplified block diagram of the tracking servo IC104 in Fig. 12-6 serves as a reminder of the circuit descriptions. The tracking segment photodiodes in the optics produce the tracking

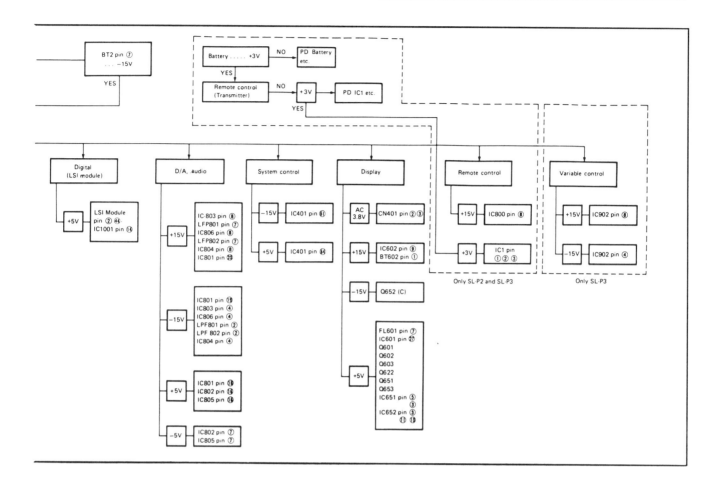

the power supply. *(Courtesy Technics)*

Fig. 12-3. Simplified key matrix for the SL-P2/P3. *(Courtesy Technics)*

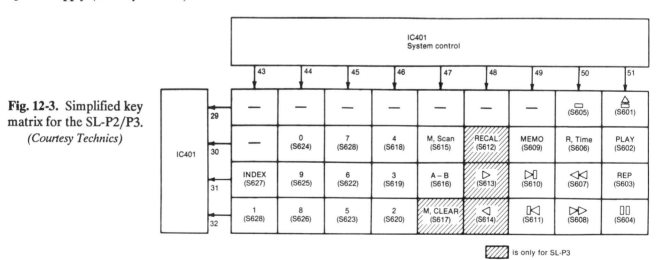

error signal. During the play mode the $\overline{\text{TR ON}}$ (tracking on) active-low signal permits the tracking error signal to control the servo loop. The $\overline{\text{THOLD}}$ (tracking hold) active-low signal is used during the search mode to keep the servo loop from overreacting to the jumping of tracks.

The KICK F/R signals are used to cause the lens to move ahead or move back, during the search modes. Table 12-1 shows the truth tables of these four controlling signals that are sent to the circuit. Notice how all four of the signals change state when the search mode is selected. The

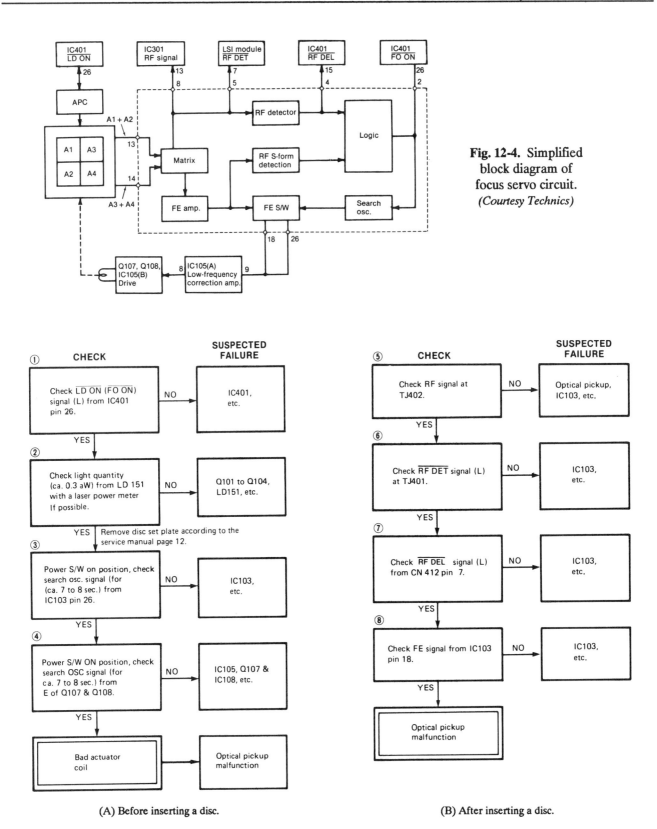

Fig. 12-4. Simplified block diagram of focus servo circuit. *(Courtesy Technics)*

(A) Before inserting a disc.

(B) After inserting a disc.

Fig. 12-5. Troubleshooting diagram for loading mechanism. *(Courtesy Technics)*

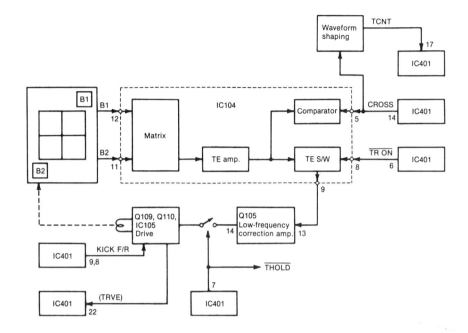

Fig. 12-6. Simplified block diagram of tracking servo circuit.

TR ON and THOLD signals will also change state when the skip mode (rapid access) is selected.

Table 12-1. Truth Table for Tracking Control
(Courtesy Technics)

	Play	Search	Skip	Stop
IC401 pin 6 (TR ON)	L	L→H	L→H	H
IC401 pin 7 (THOLD)	H	H→L	H→L	H
IC401 pin 9 (KICK F)	L	L→H	L	L
IC401 pin 8 (KICK R)	L	L→H	L	L

The operation of the circuit can be verified, first by looking to see if the tracking error signal (TE) is being generated and available at pin 9 of IC104. If this is the case, check for the presence of the CROSS signal at pin 5 of the IC, and for the presence of the TCNT (track count) signal at IC403 pin 1. If these output signals and the inputs from the system control are all present, then the tracking servo circuit is probably functioning normally. If not, then it is time to refer to the troubleshooting diagrams shown in Fig. 12-7. There are two troubleshooting diagrams, one for the failures most likely to occur during the normal playback mode, and those for the search and skip modes. Notice how each

diagram follows the signal path necessary for proper operation of tracking control IC104. This is the classic approach to troubleshooting.

CHECKING THE TRAVERSE SERVO CIRCUIT

The function of the traverse servo is to advance or retard the position of the entire optical assembly by turning the traverse motor. Criteria for determining if the traverse movement should be stepped is made by looking at the level of the tracking error drive signal. If the dc level of the error drive signal drops too far below zero, then system control IC401 will recognize that the optics must be moved forward, before the range of the tracking servo is exceeded. (This will also occur during search forward.) During search reverse, a tracking error drive signal rising too far above zero will signal IC401 to issue a REV (reverse) command. This will drive the traverse motor in the reverse direction, moving the optics in reverse. The simplified block diagram for the traverse servo can be seen in Fig. 12-8.

The first signal to check for proper operation of the traverse servo is the tracking

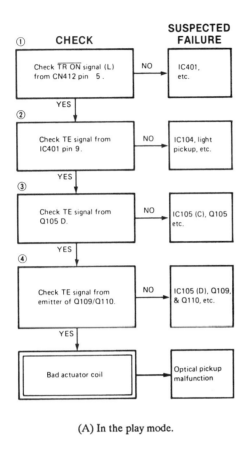

(A) In the play mode.

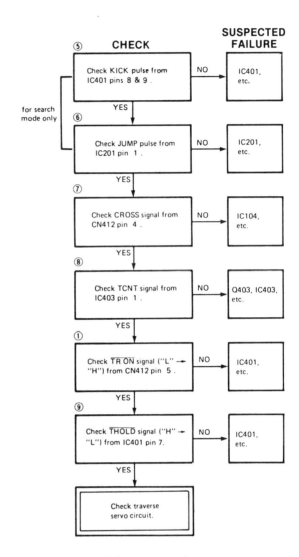

(B) In the search/skip mode.

Fig. 12-7. Troubleshooting diagrams for the tracking servo. *(Courtesy Technics)*

error drive signal, viewable at the common emitters of Q109 and Q110. This signal is low-pass filtered and then shifted in level by Q201 and Q202. This signal then becomes the TRVE signal applied to IC401 pin 22, where it can be checked. IC401 will determine if the traverse motor should be stepped forward, or backward, by issuing the FWD command at pin 28 and the REV command pin 27, respectively. The FWD signal is applied to IC201 pin 5, and the REV signal is applied to pin 6. IC201 and its associated components will drive the traverse motor. If the tracking error drive signal, TRVE, and the FWD/REV signals are present, then the operation of traverse servo is working properly.

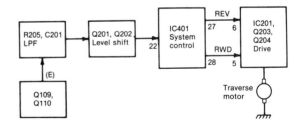

Fig. 12-8. Simplified block diagram for the traverse servo. *(Courtesy Technics)*

The FWD or REV signals can most readily be seen when the search forward/reverse mode is

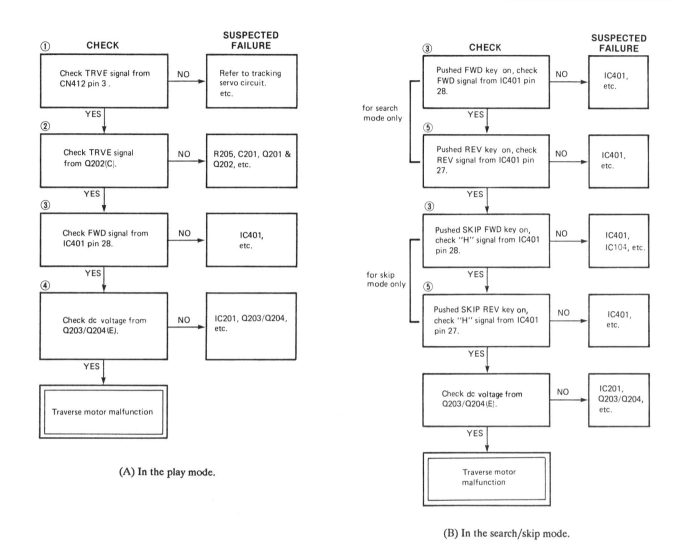

Fig. 12-9. Troubleshooting diagrams for the traverse servo. *(Courtesy Technics)*

selected. If these signals are not present, then the troubleshooting diagrams shown in Fig. 12-9 can be referred to in order to check the signal flow. As is the case for tracking servo, there are two diagrams for traverse servo, one for play and one for the search/skip modes.

CHECKING THE SPINDLE MOTOR SERVO

The simplified block diagram for the CLV servo circuit is shown in Fig. 12-10. It serves as a reminder that here are three separate loops which are used to create the error drive signal.

On start-up, the important thing is to get the spindle motor going as quickly as possible, and this the function of the constant rotation servo loop. This loop is activated when IC401 delivers its ACC (acceleration) signal. As soon as the disc is spinning at a medium speed, the spindle motor coasts for a brief period, and as soon as RF data is detected from the disc the 11T servo loop is switched in. The 11T loop criterion for servo lock is the period of the longest pit or flat length, which is 11T (10 zeros and a 1). In order for this loop to operate, it must receive the playback EFM signal from the optics. After the 11T loop has been in control for a brief period, the frame sync signal (FCLK) from playback will begin to coincide with the internally clock-derived frame

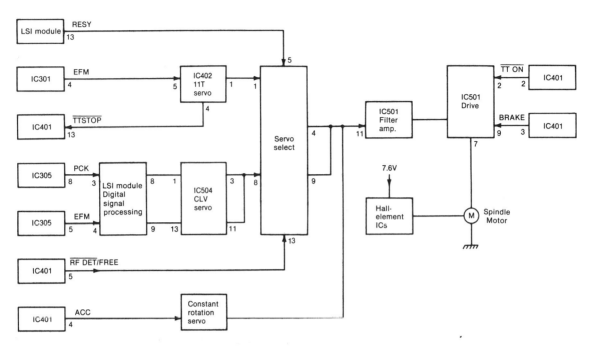

Fig. 12-10. Simplified block diagram of CLV servo. *(Courtesy Technics)*

sync signal ($\overline{\text{CLDCK}}$). At this point the CLV servo loop is switched in and the 11T loop is switched out. The CLV servo is based exactly on the coincidence of TCLK and $\overline{\text{CLDCK}}$. These signals are phase compared, and the error voltage becomes the fine error drive signal. The 11T and CLV loops are switched by IC503, an analog switch. Controlling the switching action are the FREE and RESY signals. IC501 provides the drive signal to run the spindle motor. The motor is a direct-drive type, whose position sensors (Hall-element ICs) are connected back to IC501.

The following signals must be present in order for the spindle motor servo to work. The turntable-on command, $\overline{\text{TT ON}}$ active low, must be generated by IC401, and can be checked there at pin 2. It should go low when play is pressed. The RF detection signal, $\overline{\text{RF DET}}$ active low, must be generated by IC401 in order to initiate the 11T servo. This signal can be checked at test point TJ401. This signal is necessary so that IC401 can generate the FREE signal, which causes the spindle motor to coast just before the 11T servo is switched in. The 11T servo will be switched in when the FREE signal returns to zero. The turntable-stop indicator, the $\overline{\text{TTSTOP}}$ active-low signal, must be high in order for the

spindle motor to operate, and the BRAKE signal at IC401 pin 3 similarly must be low. The $\overline{\text{TTSTOP}}$ signal is not a command from the system control IC. It is generated by IC403, at pin 7. The playback EFM signal must also be present for the 11T servo loop to operate, and this can be checked at the base of Q501. The CLV servo loop requires the presence of the FCLK and $\overline{\text{CLDCK}}$ signals from the LSI module, and it can be checked there at pins 8 and 9, respectively. Fig. 12-14 shows how the EFM, FCLK, and $\overline{\text{CLDCK}}$ signals should appear. The CLV servo loop is switched in by the RESY signal from the LSI module. It can be checked there at pin 13.

If these signals are present, and in the correct order (ACC first, FREE second, RESY third, etc.), then the spindle motor circuit is working properly. If not, then the following diagrams (Fig. 12-11) should be used for reference. Fig. 12-11A outlines the signal path that should be checked when the unit is first played from the stop condition. There are really three major parts of this diagram: failure in start-up (constant rotation), failure in 11T, and failure in CLV. Fig. 12-11B is for play-to-stop transitions, that is, if the spindle motor does not stop, or if it takes a long time to stop.

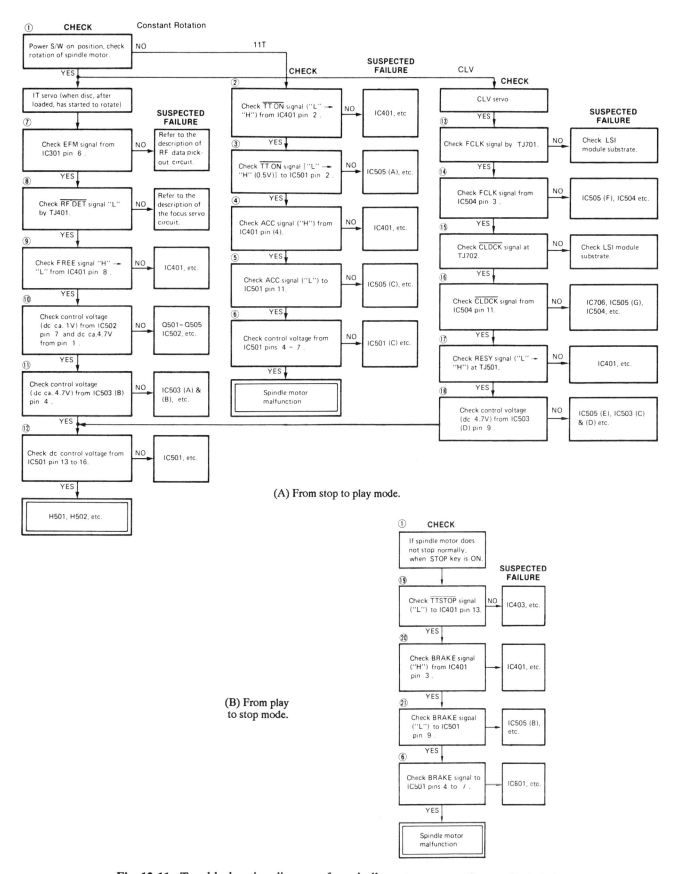

Fig. 12-11. Troubleshooting diagrams for spindle motor servo. *(Courtesy Technics)*

CHECKING THE EFM (DATA EXTRACTION) CIRCUIT

A simplified block diagram of the RF wave-shaper, PLL, and EFM detector is shown in Fig. 12-12. The playback RF data from the optics is applied to a waveshape circuit in IC301. This will square up the signal for use by the PLL circuit. The dc level of the RF signal is also regulated by a comparator stage in IC302. It operates by looking at the output of the waveshaper and then adding a compensating dc level back to its input. This is done to prevent dc level shifting of the RF signal which could be due to poor optical performance or variations in disc manufacturing. A clock signal from the LSI module, TTCK, is divided and applied to the input of the wave-shaping circuit to minimize the effect of RF dropout on the phase-locked loop. This compensated, shaped signal is then available for use by the servo circuit. To operate the PLL section, the shaped RF signal is sent to an edge detector, which produces pulses which all have the same width. The resulting signal becomes one input to the phase comparator. The output of the phase comparator is low-pass filtered and is used to drive an 8.64-megahertz VCO. The VCO output is divided and then becomes the second input to the PLL phase comparator. The VCO output is then gated to produce the EFM signal for decoding, and the PCK signal, also for decoding.

Two input signals must be present for this circuit to operate. They are the RF signal which can be checked at test point TJ402 and the TTCK signal from the LSI module at pin 17. If these two signals are present, then the EFM and PCK signals should be available at IC305 pin 5 and test point TJ301, respectively. If these signals are not present, then follow the troubleshooting diagram shown in Fig. 12-13. This diagram, like others, is prepared in order of signal flow, and suggests a faulty component as the cause.

CHECKING THE LSI MODULE

The LSI module is the one circuit in the SL-P2 which can somewhat be considered to be a black box device. It contains the three ICs which perform error correction and EFM demodulation. It is difficult to check signal flow between the three ICs within the module since they are mounted vertically. Several input and output signals, however, are required for proper LSI module operation. The two main input signals to the LSI are the EFM signal and the PCK signal, both from the EFM/PCK data extraction circuit. These two signals appear at pins 4 and 3 of the LSI module, respectively. These signals should look like those shown in Fig. 12-14. Output signals used to control other circuits include the FCLK, $\overline{\text{CLDCK}}$, and RESY signals used by the spindle motor servo circuit. These signals appear at pins 8, 9, and 13, respectively at the LSI module (Fig. 12-15). The TTCK signal, used by

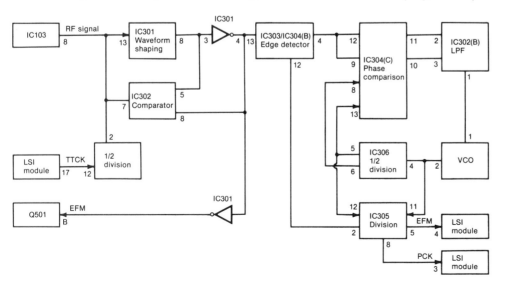

Fig. 12-12. Simplified block diagram of the data extraction circuit. *(Courtesy Technics)*

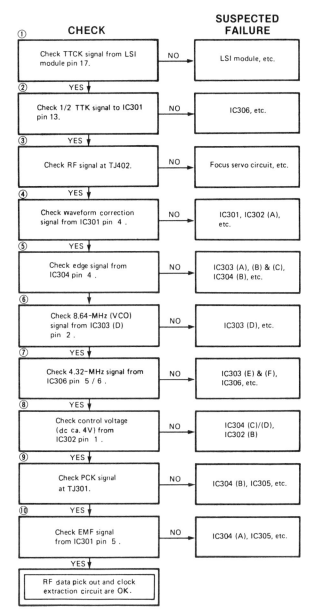

Fig. 12-13. Troubleshooting chart for the data extraction circuit. *(Courtesy Technics)*

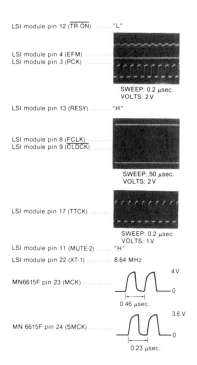

Fig. 12-14. Key voltages and waveforms found in the LSI module. *(Courtesy Technics)*

the RF waveshaping circuit, should appear at pin 17 of the module. Timing signals that are necessary for proper operation include the 8.64-megahertz crystal clock at pin 22. Counted-down clock signals MCK (2.16 megahertz) and SMCK (4.32 megahertz) should appear at pins 23 and 24, respectively, of the module. The subcode channels, primarily the Q channel, must be faithfully decoded and appear at pins 6 and 14, respectively, of the module. These signals should appear just as those shown in Fig. 12-14 during play. If they do not, refer to the troubleshoot-

ing diagram in Fig. 12-16. The diagram checks for LSI module failure with the symptom of no front-panel display and that of good display but with bad sound.

CHECKING THE D/A AND AUDIO CIRCUITS

The simplified block diagram for the D/A converter and audio circuits is shown in Fig. 12-17. The LSI module produces 16-bit-wide digital audio samples and the left and right deglitching signals necessary to obtain an analog audio stream and to deserialize the stream into separate left and right audio signals. IC801 performs the D/A conversion and deglitching is done by IC802/IC805. Two low-pass filters, LPF801 and LPF802, filter the deglitched signals to remove any remaining switching noise. The left channel is then phase shifted by IC804 to make it match the timing of the right channel. The right channel had to be delayed during recording to create a serial data stream. The final output buffers for the left and right channels

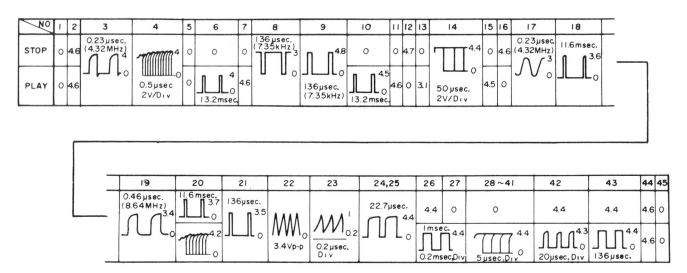

Fig. 12-15. Voltages and waveforms for the pins of the LSI module. *(Courtesy Technics)*

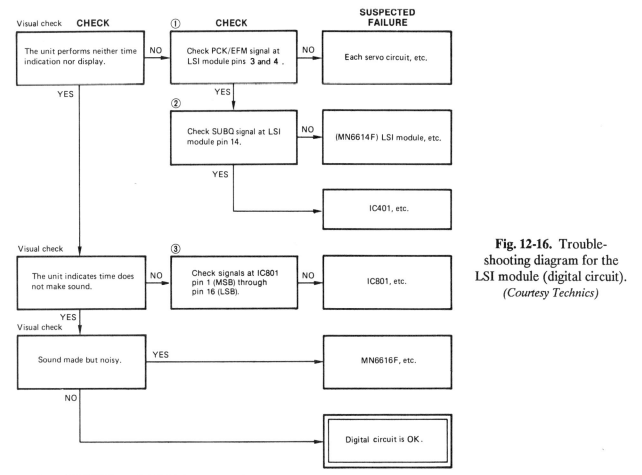

Fig. 12-16. Trouble-shooting diagram for the LSI module (digital circuit). *(Courtesy Technics)*

consist of IC804 and IC806, respectively. Extra deemphasis is performed for those CDs recorded as such, and the EMPH signal from IC401 will change the playback curves of both of the buffers. The output terminals are connected either to the output buffers or to ground, according to the action of the muting relay, which is controlled by the MUTE signal from IC401.

The 16-bit digital audio samples should be present at pins 26 through 41 of the LSI module.

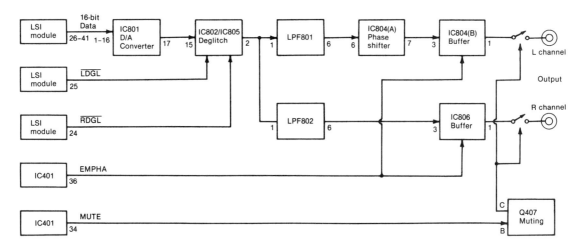

Fig. 12-17. Simplified block diagram for the D/A converter and audio circuitry. *(Courtesy Technics)*

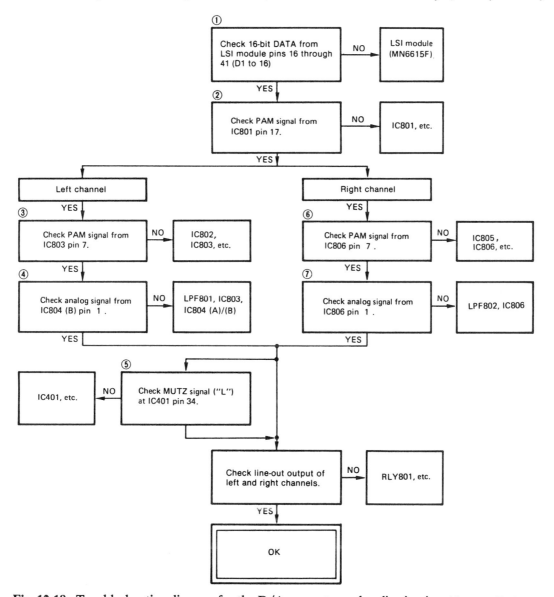

Fig. 12-18. Troubleshooting diagram for the D/A converter and audio circuits. *(Courtesy Technics)*

The right and left deglitching signals ($\overline{\text{RDGL}}$, $\overline{\text{LDGL}}$, active low) should be present at pins 24 and 25, respectively, of the LSI module. The MUTE signal at IC401 pin 34 should be low for play and search, but should be high for stop, pause, and skip. If these signals are all present as specified, then there should be good playback. If this is not the case, refer to the troubleshooting diagram shown in Fig. 12-18. The diagram lists the signal paths for the left and right channels separately.

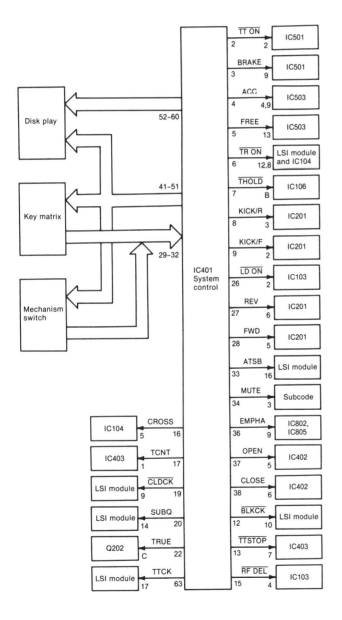

Fig. 12-19. Simplified diagram of system control IC401. *(Courtesy Technics)*

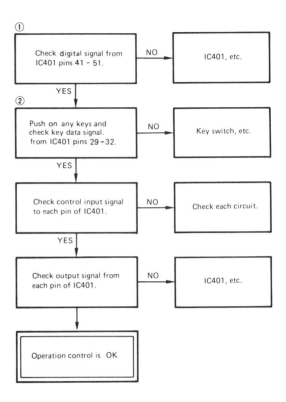

Fig. 12-20. Troubleshooting diagram for system control IC401 and associated components. *(Courtesy Technics)*

CHECKING THE SYSTEMS CONTROL IC

A simplified block diagram of system control IC401 and some associated components is shown in Fig. 12-19. This IC is the center of all activity in the unit, and checking its operation is really just a matter of confirming its inputs and outputs. IC401 is totally responsible for interpreting the Q subcode channel and calculating the data in order to drive the front-panel display. Pins 41 through 60 are used to drive the display tube, FL01. Key matrixing is tied to the IC by scanning lines 41 through 51 (also used to drive the display), and by input lines 29 through 32. A list of the key input and output signals for IC401 is shown in Chart 12-1. The troubleshooting diagram is shown in Fig. 12-20. It may seem ironic that the single most complex component in the unit has what appears to be the simplest chart. But if the chart is read more carefully, it will seem that it

Chart 12-1. Key Signals Used and Generated by System Control IC401 *(Courtesy Technics)*

Input Signals

LSI module pin 10 ($\overline{\text{BLKCK}}$)..
LSI module pin 9 ($\overline{\text{CLDCK}}$)..
LSI module pin 14 (SUBQ)..
LSI module pin 17 (TTCK)..
} From LSI module

IC403 pin 7 ($\overline{\text{TTSTOP}}$)..
} From CLV servo circuit

IC103 pin 4 ($\overline{\text{RF DEL}}$)..
} From focus servo circuit

IC104 pin 5 (CROSS)..
IC403 pin 1 (TCNT)..
} From tracking servo circuit

Q202 C (TRVE)..
} From traverse servo circuit

Output Signals

IC401 pin 2 ($\overline{\text{TT ON}}$)..
IC401 pin 3 (BREAK)..
IC401 pin 4 (ACC)..
IC401 pin 5 (FREE)..
} To CLV servo circuit

IC401 pin 6 ($\overline{\text{TR ON}}$)..
IC401 pin 7 ($\overline{\text{THOLD}}$)..
IC401 pin 8 (KICK R)..
IC401 pin 9 (KICK F)..
} To tracking servo circuit

pin 26 ($\overline{\text{LD ON}}$)..
} To focus servo circuit

IC401 pin 27 (REV)..
IC401 pin 28 (FWD)..
} To traverse servo circuit

IC401 pin 35 (SYNC)..
} At SYNCHRO REC mode (L)

IC401 pin 34 (MUTE)..
IC401 pin 36 (EMPHA)..
} To D/A converter and audio circuit

IC401 pin 37 (OPEN)..
IC401 pin 38 (CLOSE)..
} To loading mechanism

calls for checking each operation and each control and input signal associated with that operation. Certainly, if the problem with the unit is that the door won't open or close, the technician won't necessarily have to start checking the servo control signal from the IC. The chart is really useful only if the specific symptom is already known; otherwise a lot of time could be wasted checking for signals that are not related to the problem area.

CHECKING THE REMOTE CONTROL

A simplified block diagram of the remote-control transmitter and the main unit's receiver is shown in Fig. 12-21. IC1, in the transmitter, develops the wireless code and drives the infrared LED, D1. The infrared code is received by photodiode

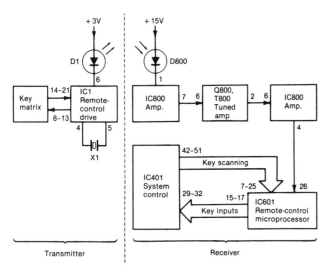

Fig. 12-21. Simplified diagram of remote-control circuit. *(Courtesy Technics)*

D800 in the main unit. The signal is amplified by IC800 and detected by Q800 and T800. This signal is then sent to IC801, the remote-control decoder microprocessor. The remote control should always be supplied with fresh batteries so that the following signals can be developed. At

IC1 pin 4, there should be a crystal-controlled high-frequency oscillator. At the collector of Q1 the code signals should be present. For the receiver side, in the main unit, the signal from photodiode D800 should be present at pin 1 of IC800. The amplified and detected signal should be presented at pin 4. These signals should appear as shown in Fig. 12-22. If these signals are not present, refer to the troubleshooting diagram shown in Fig. 12-23. This chart follows the signal path from the transmitter to the receiver and decoder microprocessor.

It is worth repeating that having the right information handy is as important as developing good troubleshooting skills. The service manual or other literature from the manufacturer or other sources is a necessary map when trying to troubleshoot any unit.

Familiarity with the normal operation of the unit in question is necessary before one can determine that a problem does exist. Studying the operating instructions or spending time with an actual unit will provide the most useful information in the least amount of time. Finally, don't let a "dog" unit bring on frustrations. There are those times in troubleshooting when a brick wall is reached–either there are so many symptoms and they are so confusing that they can't be traced or the problem is so intermittent that it pops its nasty head only when the technician has gone for a second cup of coffee. The best advice in these cases is to take a break and clear the mind for a while, and start at the problem again later. And many times, embarrassingly enough, a casual guess from a friend or fellow technician will lead one to finding the

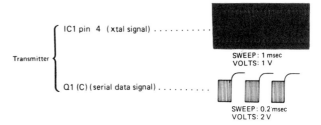

Fig. 12-22. Key signals internal to remote-control unit. *(Courtesy Technics)*

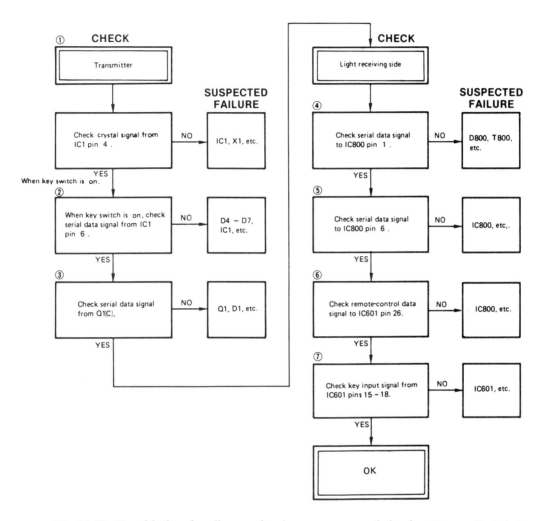

Fig. 12-23. Troubleshooting diagram for the remote-control circuit. *(Courtesy Technics)*

cause of the problem. These expedients are valid for servicing all electronic products, not just CD players. The important difference to keep in mind concerning CD players is that they represent the very latest in technology and, also, a wise investment on the part of the consumer. The consumer deserves the best service possible, simply because the customer is always right.

13

The CD-ROM

The potential of the compact disc technology is not limited to audio applications. Its ability to store mass qualities of data enables the compact disc to serve as a data bank for computers. In this capacity the disc serves the function of a read-only memory, or ROM. Within the structure of the computer system, the ROM is a fixed memory reference that feeds information to the central processing unit (CPU). The disc medium can contain the programming information. It is the amount of program information and its resistance to damage that represent the two primary advantages of CD-ROMs. The 5.25-inch (13.33-centimeter) floppy disc used in many personal computers can hold a maximum of 360 000 bytes. Special high-density type 5.25-inch floppies can hold 1.2 megabytes. A hard, or fixed, magnetic disc has a capacity ranging from 10 to 30 megabytes. This is far less than the capacity of the CD-ROM, which is 500 to 600 megabytes. The differences in capacity are a result of the density data packing. The CD-ROM houses information in pit structures in the same manner as a CD audio disc. The 0.06-micrometer pit and 1.6-micrometer bit separation yields an information density of 16 000 tracks per inch (6300 tracks per centimeter). This figure compares with a track density of 96 tracks per inch (38 tracks per centimeter) for the floppy disc and 500 tracks per inch (197 tracks per centimeter) for the fixed magnetic disc.

Unlike both the floppy and fixed magnetic discs, the CD-ROM maintains all the qualities of the CD audio disc. Information fixed on the disc can be considered permanent. Since information is read from the CD-ROM in the same manner as for the audio CD, it is safe from outside contamination and magnetic fields. Both of these could seriously impair the performance of magnetic floppy discs. The main difference between the use of floppy discs and the CD-ROM is in the inability of the CD-ROM to accept new information. Data can only be placed on the CD-ROM by the stamping process which is the same used in the manufacturing of CD audio discs. As in audio disc pressing, once the data is impressed on the CD-ROM it cannot be changed. Floppy discs, however, can accept new data which is input by the user via the computer's keyboard.

The ability of the CD-ROM top to hold mass quantities of fixed information lends it to electronic publishing. Electronic encyclopedias are a good example of this. Placing this information on CD-ROM allows users to quickly access any particular subject. Another use is that of providing financial data on corporations. Due to the inability to record over CD-ROM and the limited number of CD-ROM pressings these services are fairly expensive, ranging from $10 000 to $20 000 per year. Indeed, any reference material can lend itself to being put on CD-ROM. The list is continuing to grow. The greatest advancement to the growth of CD-ROM has not been in technology. Until the spring of 1985, no standard existed for the CD-ROM. Although all of the CDs were physically the same, they differed in their operating structures. Without any operating standards, electronic publishers were forced to develop multiple software operating systems. This is an expensive process that drove up the cost of disc production. Increased costs limited monies available for producing titles. Publishers were faced with the possibility that monies and resources would be devoted to a product that could have short production runs and could return momentary losses. It was this aspect of CD-ROMs that caused CD-ROM manufacturers and programming companies to push for standards. In the late fall of 1985, thirteen corporations met to start laying the groundwork for CD-ROM standards. This group became known as the High Sierra Group. In less than a year this group of competing companies developed standards for the table of contents and directory. These two files are the keys to operating compatibility. On May 28, 1986, the High Sierra Group released the working paper for a standard CD-ROM volume and file structure.

VOLUME STRUCTURE OF CD-ROM DATA INFORMATION

As in the case of the audio CD, the key to compatibility is the arrangement of data on the disc. Each audio CD disc, regardless of manufacturer, can be played back on any CD player because it expects to see both identification and audio information at standard positions on the disc. Without standardization of data, positioning compatibility is impossible. The

same condition is true for the CD-ROM. In the CD-ROM information is contained within a file system. We can think of the structure of these files in terms of how information is written on the disc, where the information is positioned on the disc, and, finally, how the information is taken from the disc. The software information that is responsible for writing data on the disc is known as the *logic format* and the areas of disc that information is written onto is known as the *logical sector*. The data is arranged to provide the shortest possible retrieval time. Seeking information on the disc can not only be time consuming, but the software required can be both complex and expensive. Information read in sequentially results in acceptable reading rates as well as affordable software costs. A unique logical sector number (LSN) is assigned in ascending sequences with reference to the physical address of the sections containing recorded information. The lowest number is zero and ascends with each of the next higher physical addresses. The main portion of this sector tells the CD-ROM hardware where to find the directory of the files, as well as the actual structure of the directory. The directory is a grouping of data that names files carrying information. For example, a directory could contain a filename of "Digital Audio." The directory would name the file as well as its location and size, which is expressed in terms of bytes. Its structure is somewhat similar to a book's title page and table of contents. The title page names the page, while the table of contents gives the location of information within the book as well as the total book size in terms of pages. The actual information contained within the file is found via the directory.

Prior to the writing of information on the disc, the disc must be organized into a structure that reflects the logic format. This process is not a function of the disc as much as it is the responsibility of the hardware using the disc mastering process. Finally, the data on the CD-ROM must be written in a structure that permits a computer to read the information from the disc. Although this is the function of the host computer, standardization of data file structures results in standard file structures to read this data. In some cases this may require the use of a circuit board placed in the computer that gives it the ability to read data from the CD-ROM, along with instructions on the wiring configuration between the CD-ROM and the host computer. Each of these standards applies only to the arrangement of data contained within a file. The actual physical arrangement of each of the data files is covered by a separate agreement between two of the primary CD-ROM manufacturers, Philips of Holland and Sony of Japan. Information on the disc is arranged in a similar manner as on the CD audio disc. Information is arranged in blocks of data, sync patterns, control and display, and error correction. Each of the blocks is connected by a series of merging bits.

ERROR CORRECTION

The major difference between the CD-ROM and CD audio is in their error-correction capabilities. Both types of discs are manufactured in the same way and are therefore subject to the same type of manufacturing errors. These manufacturing errors combined with normal playback servo errors result in a loss of playback data. In the audio CD the information lost in any block represents less than a quarter-second duration. Large duration losses are easily masked by reproducing the previous good section. In all, the error-correction capability of the CD audio makes playback error unnoticeable. While typical error rates of one in 10^9 are acceptable for audio CDs, this same error rate in a CD-ROM would make it impractical as a data storage device (see Fig. 13-1). When dealing with CD-ROM as opposed to other storage devices, we must keep in mind that once data is placed on the disc it cannot be altered. In CD-ROM systems the key is to avoid errors. Such devices must adhere to acceptable error rates of no more than one error byte in 10^{12} of reproduced bytes. This is the equivalent of a single-byte error read during the playback of 2000 discs. In order to reduce byte read errors to this level the CD-ROM system uses an error-correction coding system, referred

to as ECC. The system consists of two processes that work in conjunction with each other, error detection and error correction.

Error correction begins with error detection. This process consists of a number loaded in the data program known as a *check sum*. In a check sum program a series of numbers representing the data is totaled and rounded off to the closest whole number. The remaining number is the check sum and compared to a number of the same value. The check sum method is by no means foolproof. An error in two numbers could result in the correct sum and remainder. Although this possibility exists, mistakes resulting in a correct sum are unlikely. While check sum methods are useful for error correction they cannot be used to determine which of the digits is incorrect.

The correction process finds its bases in the error-detection process. From this point programming built into the integrated circuits of the CD-ROM sets down rules governing more detailed correction. These internal preprogrammed rules are called *algorithms*. The result is a cyclic redundancy check (CRC) similar to that used in the CD audio disc. The use of CRC reduces the error correction down to the resolution of single-bit errors. Now that a single-bit error has been detected and located, we can use the Hamming codes for correction. As in the audio CD disc, by adding 3 check bits to every 4 bits of data information, single-bit information can be corrected. Hamming codes are useful, provided errors are limited to single bits. Beyond this it's possible that 2-bit errors could yield a correct result. Should this occur, the Hamming codes would not be affected and data would go uncorrected. At this point the correction methods employed adequately satisfy the needs of the compact audio disc. The error-correction needs of the CD-ROM, however, require that we carry this process a step further. This is the point where error correction differs between the compact disc and the CD-ROM. CD-ROM correction takes the form of a two-layered Reed-Solomon code correction process.

In order to understand this process it is necessary to review the structure of the CD-ROM block. Each block consists of 2064 bytes,

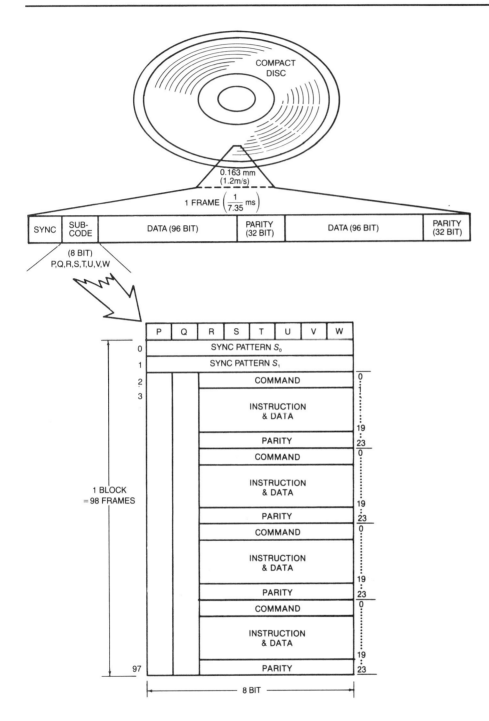

Fig. 13-1. Frame for CD-ROM with enlarged view of subcode channel. *(From Ken Pohlmann, Principles of Digital Audio, p. 260)*

of which 2048 are information data, 4 are identification, 4 are CRC bytes, and, finally, 8 bytes are 0. The 2064 bytes are then divided into 2-byte words. Each of these words, or subblocks, is portioned into one of 43 columns, each with a length of 24 rows. The bytes housed in the even and odd number columns are considered independent. As a result the total number of byte blocks is $43 \times 24 \times 2 = 2064$. The information contained at the end of each of the 43 rows is followed by 2 check bytes. In the same manner 2 check bytes are added at the end of each of the 23 rows. As a result of the addition of check bytes, the columns are increased to 45 and the rows to 26. The Reed-Solomon code can now be used to detect a single error by the cross section of its row and column. The layering of the ECC method is able to locate and correct even multiple errors since the location of each error has been identified. The combination of CIRC.

and ECC correction methods yields an error rate of 10^{13}. This satisfies the needs of the CD-ROM system.

COMPACT DISC INTERACTIVE

Compact disc interactive (CD/I) is a bridge designed to connect the data-base-only system of the CD-ROM with the entertainment capacity of the CD audio disc. It not only combines both types of functions, but adds some additional features. It also allows the reproduction of single still picture displays, or a series of pictures in animation form. This picture reproduction capability should not be confused with the ability to reproduce moving pictures. The capability to digitally reproduce moving pictures requires a lot of memory consumption. Even the amount of digital memory on the CD disc isn't enough, so displays are restricted to individual digital pictures. There are some other basic differences between CD-ROM and CD/I. CD-ROM can only operate as a computer peripheral, whereas CD/I is basically a stand-alone device. Both its operating requirements and its product features place the CD/I closer to the compact disc category than to the CD-ROM. This means that CD/I will find a place alongside the compact disc in consumer electronics stores. Its entrance into the electronics field will be aided by product standards set by both Philips and Sony.

CD/I can be looked at in terms of three separate methods of information processing: audio, video, and text.

CD/I Audio

Both compact disc and CD/I have the same capability of reproducing approximately 70 minutes plus of digital audio. The primary function of CD/I, however, isn't high-quality audio; for that, there are a number of other options. Other grades of audio with quality comparable to that of long-playing recorders or FM stereo broadcasts require less digital disc space, which results in greater playing time. On the lower end of the music-capable spectrum, playing times of up to 5 hours are possible. In a key example of CD/I's capability, pictures and audio can be combined to create a talking encyclopedia. As voice-grade audio requires the least amount of audio bandwidth, and in most cases is monophonic, CD/I disc space can handle approximately 20 hours of this type of audio.

CD/I Video

Just as in the case of audio, video on CD/I can take many forms which vary in quality. At the top end of the scale is YUV, which is sometimes referred to as delta YUV (DYUV). YUV is a European term used to describe video in its component form of luminance (brightness) and chrominance (color). This system, developed by Philips of Holland, reproduces the highest-quality video by varying the color and intensity of each pixel. The result is picture quality that matches and equals that of a broadcast video picture. This type of picture also consumes the greatest amount of memory, approximately 108 000 bytes. This limits disc storage to a maximum of 5500 high-quality pictures. In actual CD/I applications, however, the need for high-quality pictures will probably be limited. Still pictures used in association with dialogue only need to convey the thought. As a result there are three other methods of displaying pictures on CD/I. Two of the three methods display video in terms of the three primary colors, red, green, and blue (RGB). Combinations of these three primary colors can be used to create a large spectrum of secondary colors. CD/I processing can be found in two forms, each differing in resolution and required memory. The high-resolution RGB mode yields a 768- by 560-pixel picture and requires 215K of memory. Approximately 2700 of these pictures can be stored on disc. The lower RGB resolution mode creates a 384- by 280-pixel picture and a disc can store approximately 5500 pictures. The third color mode is called CLUT, for color lookup table. This mode saves memory space by limiting the amount of available colors. As a result it is limited only to reproducing graphics. It could be used to create an animated series of cartoons to accompany either audio or text. A CLUT graphic only requires 10K of memory space. At this low memory level up to 60 000 pictures can be held on disc.

CD/I Text

This is the one mode in which CD/I and CD-ROM are similar. Both can hold hundreds of millions of bytes of text. Operators of both devices can access random data as well as use the data to drive a computer.

The Drive System

Coordination for such a power tool will be a built-in computer system. The operating system used standardly by both Sony and Philips is the Motorola 68 000 series microprocessor. This same powerful IC is used in the Apple Macintosh. CD/I users will have the advantage of using it as a stand-alone system or providing fixed application programs for existing personal computers. These capabilities, as well as the mixture of data pictures, graphs, and text, may make it the universal application of compact disc technology.

Glossary

access time   When describing the ability of a CD player to quickly change selections, the time it takes to move from the track that it is on to the new track is called the access time.

address block   A permanent storage position within the memory system of a computer. This location is identified by a series of numbers.

analog   A type of electronic circuit in which the output varies directly as a function of the input. A signal state based on continuously changing physical quantities.

analog to digital   Refers to a conversion circuit used to transform analog information into digital. Describes a circuit used to transfer a continuously varying voltage into a two-stage voltage.

AND **gate**   A digital gating circuit that produces a true output only when all inputs are true.

AND gate function
$$0 \cdot 0 = 0$$
$$1 \cdot 0 = 0$$
$$0 \cdot 1 = 0$$
$$1 \cdot 1 = 1$$

angstrom   A unit used to measure wavelengths with a particular reference to the wavelength of light. A unit equal to 10^{-10} meter.

audible frequency range   The range of frequencies that a human can hear. Since hearing changes with age the measurement is taken at the average ages between 3 to 5 years, when the range of hearing is approximately 20 hertz to 20 kilohertz.

astigmatism   This is the action of a light beam being changed in shape as it passes through a curved or irregular lens. Focus error detection is achieved through astigmatism, since the returning laser beam will change from an elliptical shape to circular as it becomes more and more in focus.

beam splitter (polarizing beam splitter)   In the optical path of the laser assembly, the beam splitter is used in order to separate the beam going to the disc (sending beam) from the returning beam. The beam splitter is sensitive to the polarization of the laser light.

bias   A force applied to a device in order to establish an electronic reference. A frequency used to carry an audio signal from its processing stage to the recording head and onto the recording medium. The bias frequency is selected to achieve maximum signal transfer with minimum signal loss, due to the nonlinear characteristics of magnetic recording tape.

binary number   A number used to represent a digital state. The number can be 1 or 0 and is used to represent a true or false state.

Boolean algebra   A mathematical system developed by George Boole, a famous English mathematician. It deals with true or false statements.

Boolean symbols   Numerical symbols used in Boolean algebra. These symbols are either 0 or 1 and are used to define logical operations.

CD/I   A compact disc system which is used as part of a computer system which asks users questions and notes the correctness of answers. CD-I systems can also contain pictures and audio.

CD-ROM   A compact disc used to store computer program information. As information can only be read from the disc, it is referred to as a read-only memory (ROM) device.

CIRC (cross-interleave Reed-Solomon code)   A coding system used to correct errors that occur during digital encoding. The error correction used in digitally encoding audio signal.

collimating lens   In the optical path of the laser assembly, the collimating lens is used to keep the laser beam from diverging, i.e., to keep the beam narrow.

control block   Circuitry within a computer system designed to decode the pre-programmed instruction used to control the functions of a CPU. The area of a computer that creates control signals that carry out operating functions.

control word   This is an 8-bit nonaudio data word included with every frame that is recorded on the disc. It is used to form the subcode channels.

CAV (constant angular velocity)   Refers to a recording system used for high-performance magnetic and optical disc drives. Recorded information becomes more spread out towards the outer tracks. Although this decreases the disc storage area it simplifies speed servo operation by maintaining a constant angular speed from the inner to outer tracks.

CLV (constant linear velocity)   Refers to a system used for recording information on compact disc. This system packs the maximum amount of information on the disc. As a result the rotation speed must be changed as information is read from the inner to outer tracks in order to maintain a constant rate of reading data.

CRC (cyclic redundancy check)   An encoding and decoding system used to detect transmission errors. The system uses division to produce a remainder which is applied to the system as a check bit.

decibel   Letter symbol: dB. A standard unit of measurement used to express power level loss or gain of an electronic signal.

delta YUV   A high-quality video processing system used to describe video in its component form of luminance (brightness) and chrominance (color). This type of video processing system is used for CD/I and requires a great deal of memory.

digital signal   This is an electrical signal whose amplitude can assume only one of two values. In CD, the analog audio information is first converted to digital form before going onto the disc. Digital recording systems are superior on all counts to analog recording systems.

digital sum value   A value that represents the lengths of the pits and flats in the digital data stream. In compact disc systems the suppression of low frequency is based on minimizing the digital sum value.

digital to analog   Refers to a computer device that changes a digital, or binary, voltage to a continuous voltage.

dropout   In either analog or digital recording systems, dropout is the momentary loss of playback information. In CD, measures are taken in order to compensate for dropout.

dynamic-element matching   The range of signals between a minimum and maximum value which allows the greatest amount of signal transfer between two devices or two stages of signal processing. For compact disc systems it is used to increase the accuracy of converting a digital signal to analog.

dynamic range   The difference between the minimal acceptable level and the overload level of an electronic signal processing system.

EFM (eight- to fourteen-bit modulation)   A signal process used for encoding information for compact discs. The expansion from 8 to 14 bits permits the additions of error check bits and correcting bits, decreasing signal losses. The most important function of EFM is to limit the high-frequency content of the data stream.

encoding   The transfer of information, usually in analog form, into a digital signal, without any information loss.

equalization   Signal processing system which maintains signal amplitude and phase over a broad range of frequencies. Circuitry that compensates for the tendency of higher frequencies to be attenuated.

father   A metal stamp that is used to print the physical impressions that represent digital signal pits on a master stamping disc which is used for the actual pressing of the individual CD. The father is sometimes also referred to as the master.

fidelity   The degree that a system or a part of a system reproduces an output signal with the same characteristics of its input.

flag   Refers to a bit that holds information which indicates that a decision has been reached to a condition is present. Flags are used in error corrects and modulation processes of CD signal processing.

flats   Physically smooth areas that project out from the surface area of the compact disc. The manner that they reflect the light projected by the laser is translated into an electronic digital signal.

flutter   Frequency deviations that are created by transport irregularities. This distorts playback quality. Flutter is usually used to refer to frequency deviations at above 10 hertz.

flux density   The amount of signal that can be accepted on a specific area of a recording medium. In tape recording, the amount of signal that can be recorded on a specific area of tape.

focus lens   This is the final element in the laser optical assembly. The focus lens focuses the laser beam onto the disc.

focus servo   A control system that is used to accurately project the laser's light on the CD surface flats and pits. This results in how well the signal is read, and the quality of the reproduced CD audio.

frame   A unique string of bits containing 588 bits including sync words, subcode audio data, parity, and audio words.

frequency   The number of occurrences of a particular signal in a period of 1 second. The usual symbol for frequency is f.

frequency response   A measurement that determines how well a circuit outputs a range of frequencies applied to it. For audio devices, frequency response is the measurement of amount of signal loss from the low to high end of the audible frequency range.

grating lens   In a three-beam system, the grating lens, located in the laser optical path, is responsible for creating three separate beams from the one beam which is emitted from the laser diode.

Hamming code   A coding system used to check and correct errors in the EFM process. A type of data code that can be automatically checked.

head gap   The space inserted into an electromagnetic recording head which forces or directs magnetic flux lines onto a recording medium. The manufacturing limitations of the head gap size in part account for high-frequency recording limitations.

hertz   Letter symbol: Hz. A term used to describe the unit of frequency which is equal to the number of cycles occurring in 1 second.

hum   A type of distortion which occurs when the power supply is not properly grounded. As a result, variations in the power leak into the signal amplification process, causing poor signal reproduction.

inductive reactance   A type of resistance to alternating current. As the frequency increases, so does the inductive reactance. This creates a difficulty in maintaining frequency response in audio equipment.

interleaving   An encoding process used in converting analog audio to digital audio. A process of mixing up the data information so that any defects in the encoding or playback process will not occur over consecutive bits.

interpolation   This is the name of the operation of filling in missing information (dropouts) with an average value of the two data points located on either side of the dropout.

land   When the master CD disc is cut, the laser will cut a pit when energized, and it will not cut when it is deenergized. The space on the disc between pits is called a land or a flat.

laser   A device that takes an incoherent light source and obtains from it an extremely narrow and intense beam of coherent light. It is the heart of the compact disc system. The laser is used to read the differences in the bits and flats which represent the audio signal.

least significant digit   Abbreviated LSD. The digit carrying the lowest weight in a binary number.

main beam   In a three-beam system, the center and strongest beam is called the main beam. It is used to read the pits in order to develop audio data.

master disc   The first disc that is created by the process of transforming the analog signal to digital form and imprinting it on the disc. Sometimes the master disc is also referred to as the father.

merging bit   A bit used to tie together the various sections of a frame.

metal-oxide semiconductor   Abbreviated MOS. A type of integrated circuit chip used in computer systems particularly for high-speed memory and read-only memory.

microsecond   One-millionth of a second (10^{-6} second).

most significant digit   Abbreviated MSD. The digit with the highest weight in a binary number.

mother   A positive disc which is stamped from the father and which in turn is used to produce the negative stampers.

NAND   A logic operation that works opposite to that of an AND function. If at least one of the input statements is false, the output statement is true.

NAND gate function
0 NAND 1 = 1
1 NAND 0 = 1
0 NAND 0 = 1
1 NAND 1 = 0

nonreturn to zero   Abbreviated nrz. A method of recording signals on compact disc during which the state of the medium corresponds to the binary state of the incoming signal. The state of the medium changes every time the signal changes from 0 to 1 or 1 to 0.

nonreturn to zero inverted   Abbreviated nrzi. The process opposite to nonreturn to zero (nrz).

NOR gate   A circuit whose output is high only when all its inputs are low. Its output is the inverse of the OR gate.

NOR gate function
0 NOR 1 = 0
1 NOR 0 = 0
0 NOR 0 = 1
1 NOR 1 = 0

OR gate   A logic gate with the property that if one of the inputs is positive, the output will be positive.

OR gate function
0 + 0 = 0
0 + 1 = 1
1 + 0 = 1
1 + 1 = 1

parity bit (word)   A bit (or word) used to check that data has been correctly transmitted accurately.

P channel   A series of bits within the frame that informs the compact disc system as to the location of the lead in, lead out, and play areas of the disc.

permeability   This is a measurement which compares how much better a given material is than air as a path for magnetic flux. The permeability of tape determines how long it will maintain a signal after exposure to magnetic fields.

pitch   The differences in the way we sense sounds on an ordered scale from high to low or from low to high. Pitch is also defined as the distance between two peaks or flats on adjacent tracks on a disc.

pits   The indented areas of the compact disc surface. The transitions between pits and flats create digital state changes from 1 to 0 and from 0 to 1.

polarization   Simply stated, polarization describes the orientation of the laser light energy. Laser light waves can be oriented in a horizontal, vertical, or even a circular direction.

pulse-code modulation   Abbreviated PCM. An analog-to-digital signal conversion system which makes use of the amplitude and time or phase of the audio signal to create a series of ones and zeros.

quantization   The digital sampling of the audio signal at a given instant of time.

Q channel   This channel provides information which is usually used by the digital front-panel display of a compact disc player. The channel contains mainly timing information in the form of track numbers, index numbers, the mount of time within the track in minutes, seconds, and frames, and the amount of time since the first track. It also contains the disc's table of contents.

random-access memory   Abbreviated RAM. A memory circuit which allows access to any point within its memory. As a result, information can be written in or read out very quickly.

random errors   Relatively short errors which can occur in a signal pattern. They are separated during digital processing for correction or concealment.

R-DAT   A type of digital audio recording system which uses a rotating set of heads to record the signal on tape.

read-only memory   Abbreviated ROM. An integrated circuit used to hold the fixed program of a microprocessor system.

Reed-Solomon code   An error-correcting code which is particularly effective in the correction of burst errors which happen during the analog-to-digital conversion process. A type of Reed-Solomon code known as cross interleave is used for encoding for compact discs.

reluctance   The resistance to the flow of magnetic lines of force.

revolutions per minute   Abbreviated rpm. The number of revolutions a disc rotates in 1 minute. Systems with higher revolutions per minute are usually capable of reproducing higher frequencies.

RF signal   When the laser beam reads the pits of a disc, it is then reflected back to the photodiode array, where it will develop a playback signal. This playback signal is a combination of nine different sine waves, each at a different frequency. This combination of high-frequency sine waves is called the playback RF signal.

sampling rate   The specific period during which a signal is observed. The rate at which an analog signal is transformed into a digital signal.

search   This is one of the features of a CD player. It allows a user to scan the disc quickly while the search button is being pressed.

sine wave   A signal representation which is expressed as a sine of a linear function of time.

single-beam system   Many new CD players do not rely on three beams to obtain both RF data recovery and tracking information. These systems accomplish both by using just one beam.

skip   This is a feature of a CD player. It is the ability to jump quickly to the beginning of a new track and commence playing.

Society of Motion Picture and Television Engineers   Abbreviated SMPTE. An organization of professional film and television engineers which helps determine standards for their respective industries.

spindle   The platform on which the CD is placed when it is played. It is sometimes called the turntable.

stampers   Products of the final part of the mastering process. The stampers are used to press the compact discs.

subcode   Information other than the audio data. The P and Q channels are examples of subcodes.

table of contents   Abbreviated TOC. A coding system at the beginning of a compact disc which lists the number of selections, duration of each selection, and total disc running time.

three-beam system   The optical system employed by many CD players in which there are three separate laser beams. Although they are generated from just one laser diode, two of the beams are used for tracking, and the other is used for audio data (RF) recovery.

time index numbers   Individual track selections on a disc are sometimes further subdivided for the convenience of the user. These units are called index numbers or indexes.

turntable   *See* Spindle.

two-to-ten rule   A term used to describe the function of the eight-bit to fourteen-bit modulation (EFM) stage. There can be no less than 2 but no more than 10 zeros between ones in the data stream.

wavelength   In a sine wave the distance between two points of corresponding phase on two consecutive cycles.

waveplate   In the laser optical path, the waveplate is used to alter the polarization of the beam (or beams). Each pass of a beam through the waveplate changes the polarization by 45°. Therefore a beam returning from the disc will have passed through the waveplate twice, for a total polarization change of 90°. It is this 90° shift in the polarization of the beam which allows the beam splitter to differentiate between the sending and returning beams.

wow   Distortion caused by changes of speed in a rotating disc. The term is usually used for low-frequency distortions.

Index

148 *Index*